THE ROOTS OF LANGUAGE SERIES

Wordbuilding

Learning About Roots and Prefixes

BY JOAN ROBINSON

Fearon Teacher Aids
a division of
David S. Lake Publishers
Belmont, California

Gratitude is extended to Barbara Morris, art teacher in Ridgewood, New Jersey, for her creative ideas upon which many of the illustrations for these pages are based.

Illustrator: Marilynn Barr

ISBN 0-8224-7450-6

Printed in the United States of America

1. 9 8 7 6 5 4 3 2 1

Contents

Introduction

More than 450 million people around the world speak English. (The only language used by more people is Mandarin Chinese.) English is an amalgam of many other languages, including French, Spanish, German, Dutch, Italian, Swedish, Norwegian, and Arabic. Nearly 60 percent of English words, however, are derived from Latin directly, or indirectly through Old French. Greek has also had a strong influence on English because many Latin words are ultimately derived from Greek, an earlier language than Latin. Much of our scientific and mathematical language has been coined from Greek elements.

Acquainting your students with Latin and Greek prefixes and roots will help them decode new words wherever they encounter them—in stories or in social studies or science texts (an octopus has eight legs, so an octagon must have eight sides). This knowledge will also help them use words precisely. They'll know the difference between precede and proceed, emigrant and immigrant, and deductive and inductive.

How to Use This Book

This vocabulary program, which can be used with students from grade 4 to grade 9, is the result of 18 years of teaching experience. Each of the 30 lessons is self-contained on two reproducible pages. The first page introduces a common Latin or Greek prefix or root with

- a list of five to six words—some familiar, some new, but none obscure—that use the prefix or root,
- the most common definition of each word, and
- illustrations that bring the words to life.

The second page contains exercises to help students master the prefix or root and the words introduced on the first page. Sections A and B help the students become familiar with the root or prefix and to review the definitions of the words. Section C activities require creativity and critical thinking.

A pretest shows students what they have to learn. Three review tests along the way give them practice using their new prefix- and root-based vocabulary. There is also a final test using words and prefixes from the entire book. The answer key at the end of the book includes the answers for all the exercise pages and all the tests. To help your class understand how Latin and Greek elements were incorporated into English, see the following section, "A Brief History of the Greek and Latin Roots of English."

In addition to giving your students the reproducible worksheets, you might use the words in spelling quizzes or have the students write them out phonetically. Used at the rate of one lesson or test a week, this book can take you through the entire year. However you choose to use *Wordbuilding*, your students are sure to benefit from gaining familiarity with the roots of language.

A Brief History of the Greek and Latin Roots of English

Scholars explain the prevalence of Latin and Greek elements in the English language by looking at English history. In A.D. 43 the Romans (who took much of their language from the Greeks) conquered the Celts of Britain and held power until the middle of the 400s. In spite of their resistance, the Celts adopted some Latin words during those centuries.

When the Germanic tribes—the Jutes, the Angles, and the Saxons—invaded Britain in the fifth century, they brought more Latin-based words. These words had been incorporated into the Germanic languages when the Romans visited the lands of these tribes on the European continent. Many of these were practical words—such as *cheese*, *butter*, *pound*, and *inch*—for products and concepts that the Romans introduced to the Germanic tribes.

With the spread of Christianity in the British Isles in the 600s came a whole host of Latinate words—such as *monk*, *creed*, *verse*, *temple*, and *candle*—because Latin was the language of the Church.

When the Normans, led by William the Conqueror, invaded England in 1066, they brought their French language, which came from Latin, and added some 10,000 words to English—words of nobility and feudalism, such as *palace*, *throne*, *enemy*, *army*, *soldier*, *castle*, *fashion*, and *beauty*.

In the fifteenth century, the Renaissance revived the Greek and Roman classics, which became more widely available because of the invention of the printing press. Latin became almost a second language for scholars and scientists. To be taken seriously, they had to write their books in Latin. (Today, lawyers and doctors still use Latin.) Not surprisingly, Latin words poured into the English language during the Renaissance.

To explore the history of the English language further, consult an encyclopedia or any of the following books:

Burriss, Eli E., and Lionel Casson. *Latin and Greek in Current Use.* 2d ed. Englewood Cliffs, NJ: Prentice Hall, 1949.

Ernst, Margaret S. *Words: English Roots and How They Grow.* 3d ed. rev. New York: Knopf, 1957.

Funk, Wilfred. *Word Origins and Their Romantic Stories.* 1950. Reprint. New York: Bell, 1978 .

Morris, William, and Mary Morris. *Morris Dictionary of Word and Phrase Origins.* New York: Harper and Row, 1977.

Paisner, Milton. *One Word Leads to Another: A Light History of Words.* New York: Dembner Books, 1982.

Sarnoff, Jane. *Words: A Book About the Origins of Everyday Words.* New York: Scribner, 1981.

The following dictionaries provide useful etymologies for individual words:

American Heritage Dictionary of the English Language. Ed. William Morris. Boston: Houghton Mifflin, 1969.

Webster's New World Dictionary, 2d college ed. Ed. David B. Guralnik. New York: Prentice Hall, 1986.

Webster's Ninth New Collegiate Dictionary. Ed. Frederick C. Mish. Springfield, MA: Merriam-Webster, 1985.

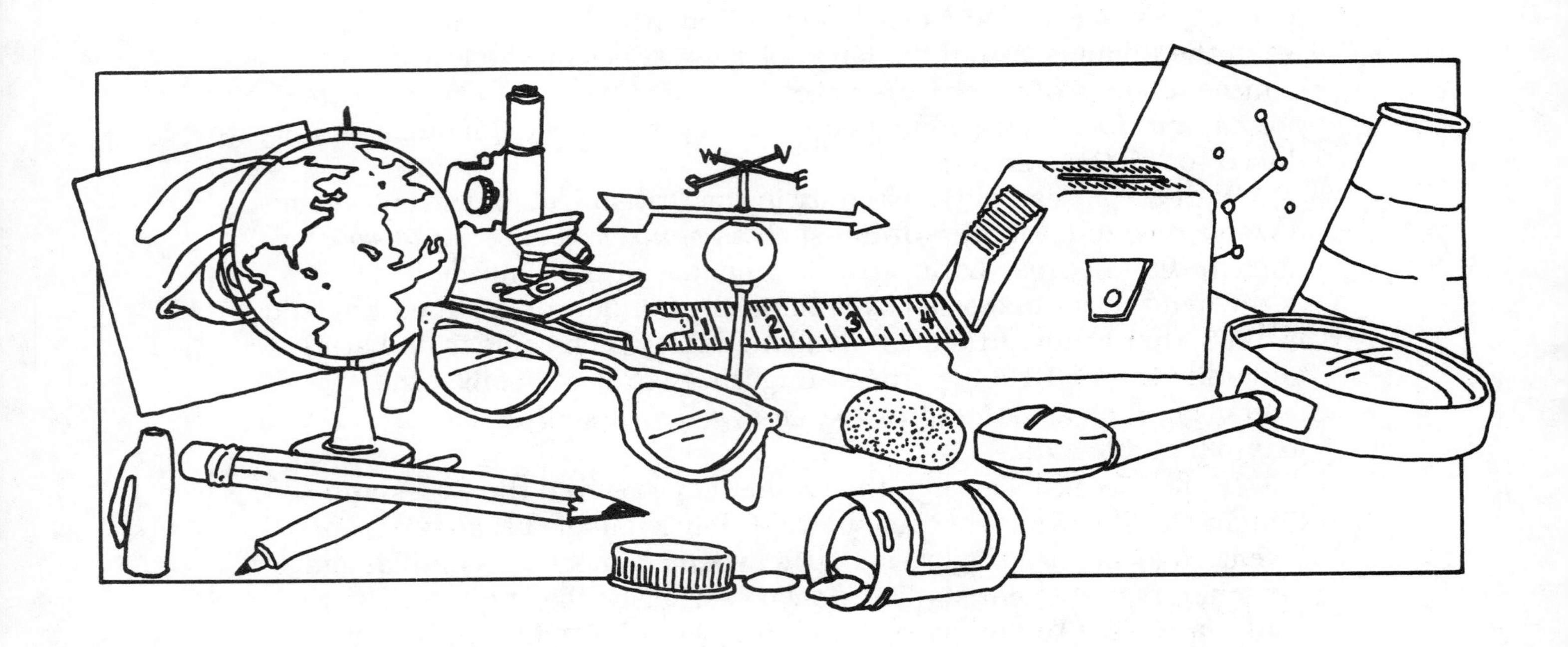

Name ____

Pretest

How many of the prefixes and roots in this book do you already know? Circle the correct answer in each sentence below.

1. *Anti* in *antiaircraft* means **for against toward.**
2. *Aqua* in *aquarium* means **fish land water.**
3. *Astro in astronaut* means **star far sight.**
4. *Audi* in *audiovisual* means **to see to move to hear.**
5. *Auto* in *autobiography* means **writing whole self.**
6. *Contra* in *contradict* means **opposite again same.**
7. *Dict* in *dictate* means **to write to say to hear.**
8. *Extra* in *extracurricular* means **beyond less than equal.**
9. *Geo* in *geography* means **map water earth.**
10. *Graph* in *mimeograph* means **to study to see to write.**
11. *Hyper* in *hyperactive* means **overly under completely.**
12. *Logy* in *archeology* means **writing the sound of the study of.**
13. *Magni* in *magnify* means **large small pretty.**
14. *Man* in *manicure* means **human color hand.**
15. *Meter* in *speedometer* means **to measure to move to write.**
16. *Multi* in *multimillionaire* means **a few some many.**
17. *Ped* in *centipede* means **worm foot eye.**
18. *Phone* in *microphone* means **sound loud speech.**
19. *Post* in *postscript* means **mail after short.**
20. *Pre* in *prehistoric* means **before after again.**
21. *Re* in *redecorate* means **before after again.**
22. *Scope* in *microscope* means **to write to look to hear.**
23. *Scrip* in *prescription* means **to write to look to hear.**
24. *Spec* in *spectator* means **to see to study to write.**
25. *Sub* in *submarine* means **below above through.**
26. *Super* in *supernatural* means **better than more than less than.**
27. *Tele* in *telescope* means **big little far.**
28. *Terra* in *terrestrial* means **sky earth water.**
29. *Un* in *undesirable* means **not partly very.**
30. *Vis* in *invisible* means **to wear to see to write.**

anti- against

antiaircraft	designed for defense against air attack
antibiotic	a substance that kills germs
antidote	a substance that counteracts poison
antifreeze	a substance that prevents liquid from freezing
antiseptic	a substance used to prevent bacteria or germs that cause decay
antisocial	withdrawn from, or hostile to, other people or to social institutions

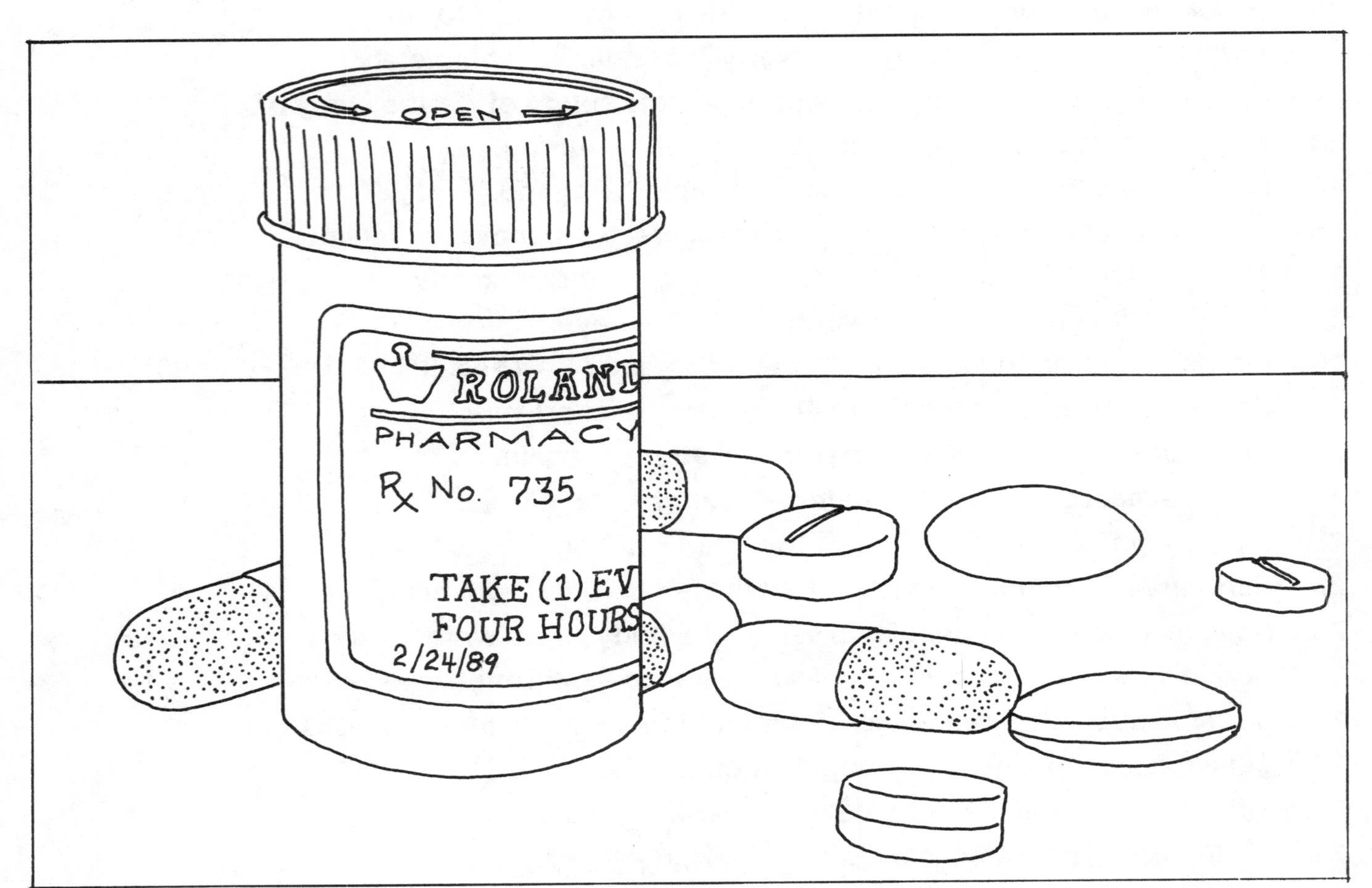

Name ______________________________

anti-

A. Circle the words that use *anti* as a prefix meaning "against." (Hint: try crossing out *anti* to see if a word is left.)

antic	antifreeze	antiquity
anticipate	antigravity	antiseptic
anticlimax	antipoetic	antisocial
antidemocratic	antique	antisymmetric

B. From the word list, select the word that best completes each sentence. Write the word in the blank.

1. During World War II, ________________ weapons were used against enemy planes.
2. Dad always puts ________________ in the car before the winter chill sets in.
3. Vandalism is ________________ behavior.
4. When Julie had pneumonia, the doctor prescribed an ________________ .
5. The child accidentally took some poison, so the doctor gave him an

   ________________ .

C. Do the following activities on separate sheets of paper.

1. Write a short paragraph about someone who behaves in an antisocial way.
2. Design an electronic game in which antibiotics kill germs.

aqua, aque water

aqualung	breathing equipment for underwater swimming or diving
aquamarine	a bluish sea-green color
aquaplane	a wide board that is towed by a motorboat, like a single water ski
aquarium	an artificial pond or tank of water where live water animals and water plants are kept; a building where such collections are exhibited
aquatic	growing or living in water
aqueduct	a channel that carries large amounts of water

Name ______________________________

aqua, aque

A. Divide the following words into parts so that *aqua* (or *aque*) is separate.

Example: aquarium aqua rium

1. aquamarine ________ ____________
2. aqualung ________ ____________
3. aquaplane ________ ____________
4. aqueduct ________ ____________

B. From the word list, select the word that best completes each sentence. Write the word in the blank.

1. To go scuba diving, you need to wear an ______________.
2. The children bought a variety of fish for the ______________.
3. Seaweed is an ______________ plant.
4. The Romans used an ______________ to transport water from one place to another.
5. Susan liked to waterski, but her brother John preferred to use an ______________.

C. Do the following activities on separate sheets of paper.

1. Write a paragraph about the kinds of plants and animals you would collect if you had a giant aquarium.
2. Draw a deluxe aquaplane skimming on top of aquamarine water.

aster, astro   star

asteroid	one of the many small planets between Mars and Jupiter
asterisk	a starlike figure (*) used to indicate footnotes or references
astrology	the study of the possible influence of the stars on people in order to predict the future
astronaut	a person who travels in space
astronomy	the science of the planets and stars

Name ______________________________

aster, astro

A. Match each word with its definition. Put the number of the definition in the blank by the word.

____ astronaut	1. scientific observation of the planets and stars
____ astrology	2. a symbol shaped like a star
____ asterisk	3. a space traveler
____ asteroid	4. the study of how the movement of heavenly bodies affect people
____ astronomy	5. tiny planets in our solar system

B. Below are definitions for variations of words on the word list. Write the new word in the blank following the definition. Then write the new word's part of speech.

Definition	*Word*	*Part of Speech*
1. a scientist who studies the planets and stars	____________	____________
2. the science that deals with travel to outer space	____________	____________
3. someone who foretells the future by studying the stars and planets	____________	____________

C. Do the following activities on separate sheets of paper.

1. Use an encyclopedia or other reference book to help you draw a picture of the solar system. Show where the asteroids are found.
2. Write a paragraph about why you would or would not like to be an astronaut.

audi — to hear

audible	loud enough to be heard
audience	the group of people attending or listening to something, especially a movie, a concert, or a play
audiovisual	involving the use of both sight and sound
audition	a trial performance in which a musician or actor is heard and evaluated
auditorium	a large theater or concert hall
auditory	having to do with hearing

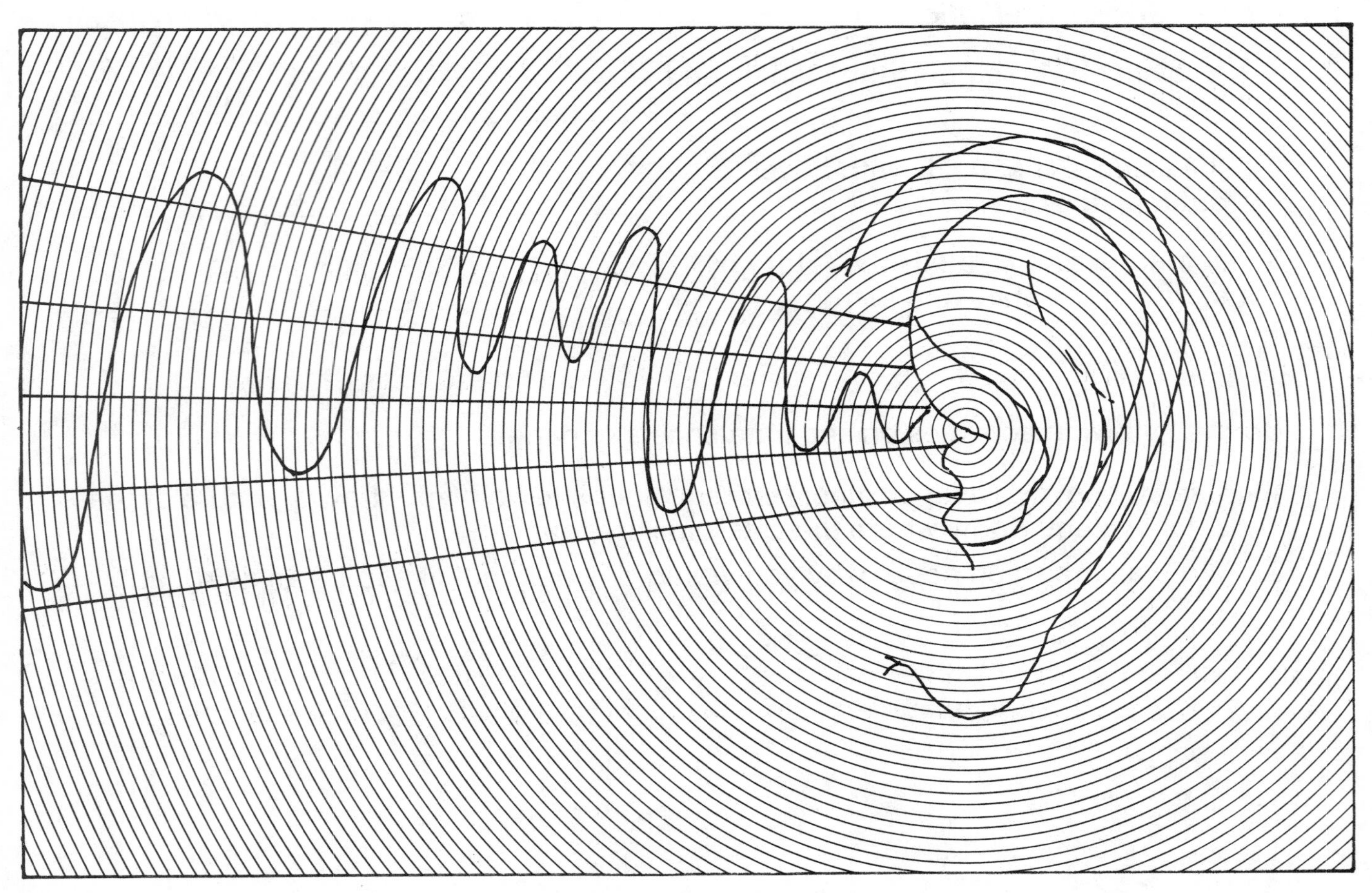

Name ______________________________

audi

A. Unscramble the word and write the definition.

Example: ceneidua   *audience*   *group of people listening to something*

1. lavusioidua ____________ ____________________
2. rotyidua ____________ ____________________
3. ibeluad ____________ ____________________
4. dumiuatiro ____________ ____________________
5. itionaud ____________ ____________________

B. From the word list, select the word that best completes each sentence. Write the word in the blank.

1. All the students poured into the ____________ for a pep rally.
2. Video monitors and film projectors are ____________ equipment.
3. Kathy was so nervous that she didn't sleep a wink the night before her ____________ for the school play.
4. My dad wants me to keep my radio turned down so low that it's barely ____________ .

C. Do the following activities on separate sheets of paper.

1. Look up *ear* in an encyclopedia or illustrated dictionary. Draw a diagram. Label the inner ear, outer ear, middle ear, auditory canal, Eustachian tube, and cochlea. Color the auditory canal.
2. Write a paragraph about being a member of an audience. This paragraph can describe either an experience you have had or one you would like to have.

auto- self

autobiography	the story of a person's life written by that person
autograph	a person's signature or handwriting
automatic	having a self-acting or self-regulating mechanism; done without thought or conscious effort
automobile	a passenger vehicle with its own engine
autonomous	self-governing

Name ______________________________

auto-

A. Name the part of speech for each of the following words.

Example: autobiography _noun_

autobiographical _adjective_

1. automobile ______________
2. automotive ______________
3. automatic ______________
4. automatically ______________
5. autonomous ______________
6. autonomy ______________

B. From the word list, select the word that best completes each sentence. Write the word in the blank.

1. The writer finished the ______________ about her life.
2. Sally got an ______________ camera for her birthday.
3. Jose was excited when he got the celebrity's ______________ .
4. The people who lived on the island did not wish to be governed by a mother country any longer. They wanted to be ______________ .

C. Do the following activities on separate sheets of paper.

1. Write an autobiographical paragraph about an event in your life.
2. Draw an automobile of the future that is fueled by something other than gasoline.

contra-, contro- against

contraband	any articles forbidden to be brought into or taken out of a country
contradict	to say the opposite; disagree
contrary	opposite or opposed; perverse or willful
contrast	to compare by showing differences *(verb);* an obvious difference *(noun)*
controversy	a difference of opinion that lasts a long time about an important matter

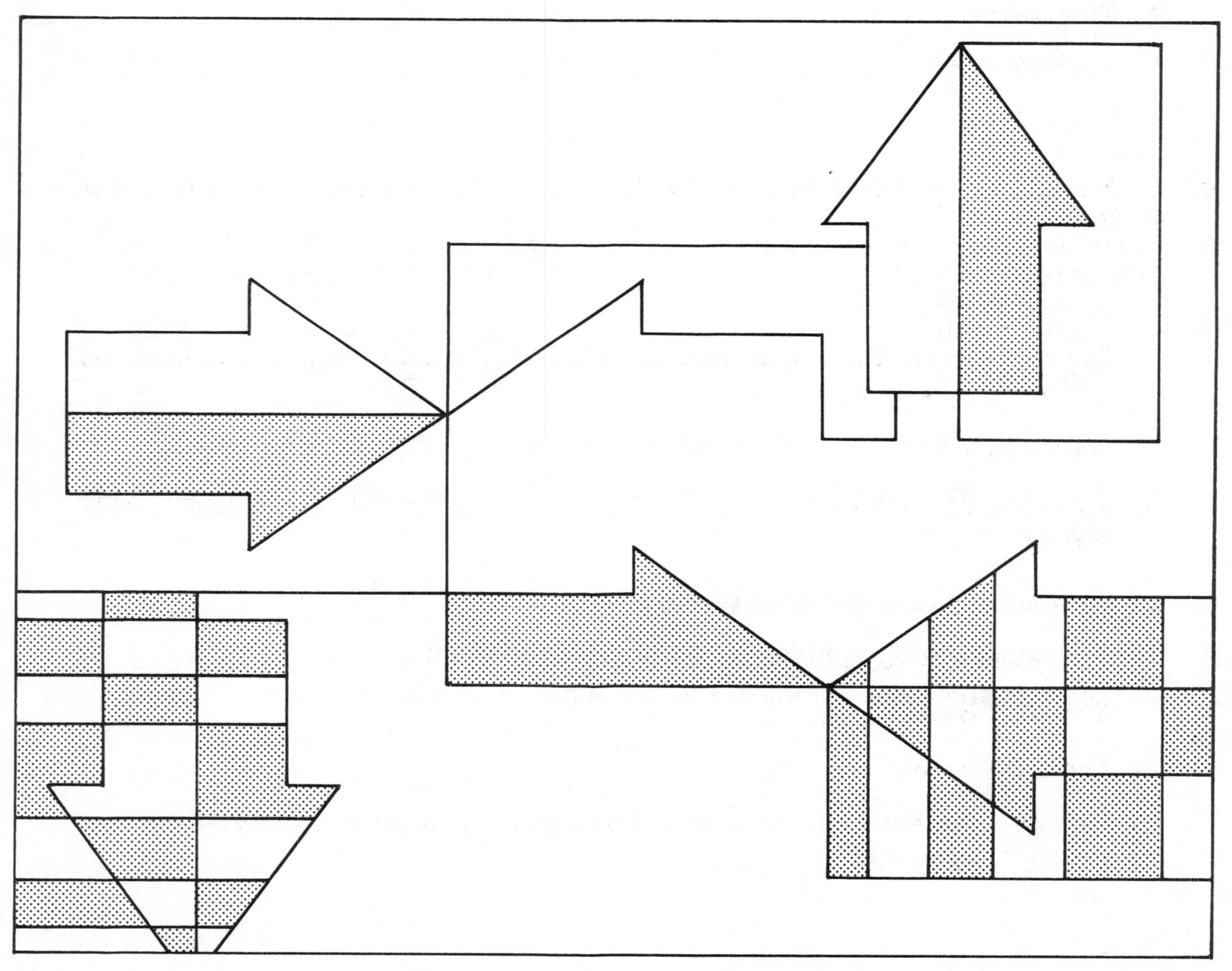

Name ____________________

contra-, contro-

A. Give the part of speech and a short definition of each word.

Example: contrary *adjective* *opposite or opposed; perverse or willful*

1. contradict ________ ____________________
2. contradiction ________ ____________________
3. contradictory ________ ____________________
4. controversy ________ ____________________
5. controversial ________ ____________________

B. From the word list, select the word that best completes each sentence. Write the word in the blank.

1. For many years a ____________ raged in the family about Grandpa Johnson's will.
2. During the Civil War, a slave who was smuggled into the North was considered ____________ .
3. Mary was quite ____________ ; she never could agree with anyone.
4. You know I never like to ____________ anyone, but you are wrong once again.

C. 1. Write a contradiction for each statement.

The weather is cold. ____________________

The pizza is hot. ____________________

The dress is old. ____________________

2. On a separate sheet of paper, write a paragraph contrasting two television shows that you watch.

dict to say

dictate	to say something aloud that will be written or recorded by another; to command or order
dictator	a ruler with unlimited power
diction	a style of speaking; the degree of preciseness or clarity in speech
predict	to foretell or say ahead of time that something will happen
verdict	a judgment or decision, especially that of a jury in a court case

Name ____

dict

A. Circle the root that means "to say" in the following words.

1. diction
2. predict
3. dictator
4. verdict

B. From the word list, select the word that best completes each sentence. Write the word in the blank.

1. The foreman of the jury announced the ________________: not guilty.
2. The actor was very careful of his ________________ during the audition.
3. The manager will ________________ the new rules to the employees.
4. I ________________ that my little brother will have a dent in his new bike before the end of the week.

C. Do the following activities on separate sheets of paper.

1. Write a paragraph about what you would do if you were a dictator.
2. Draw a picture of what you predict you will look like twenty years from now.

extra- beyond, outside

extracurricular	outside the regular school program; not part of the normal curriculum
extraneous	not essential, irrelevant
extraordinary	unusual, remarkable
extrasensory	beyond the range of normal senses
extraterrestrial	located or occurring outside the earth and its atmosphere
extravagant	wasteful, especially with money; exceeding reasonable limits

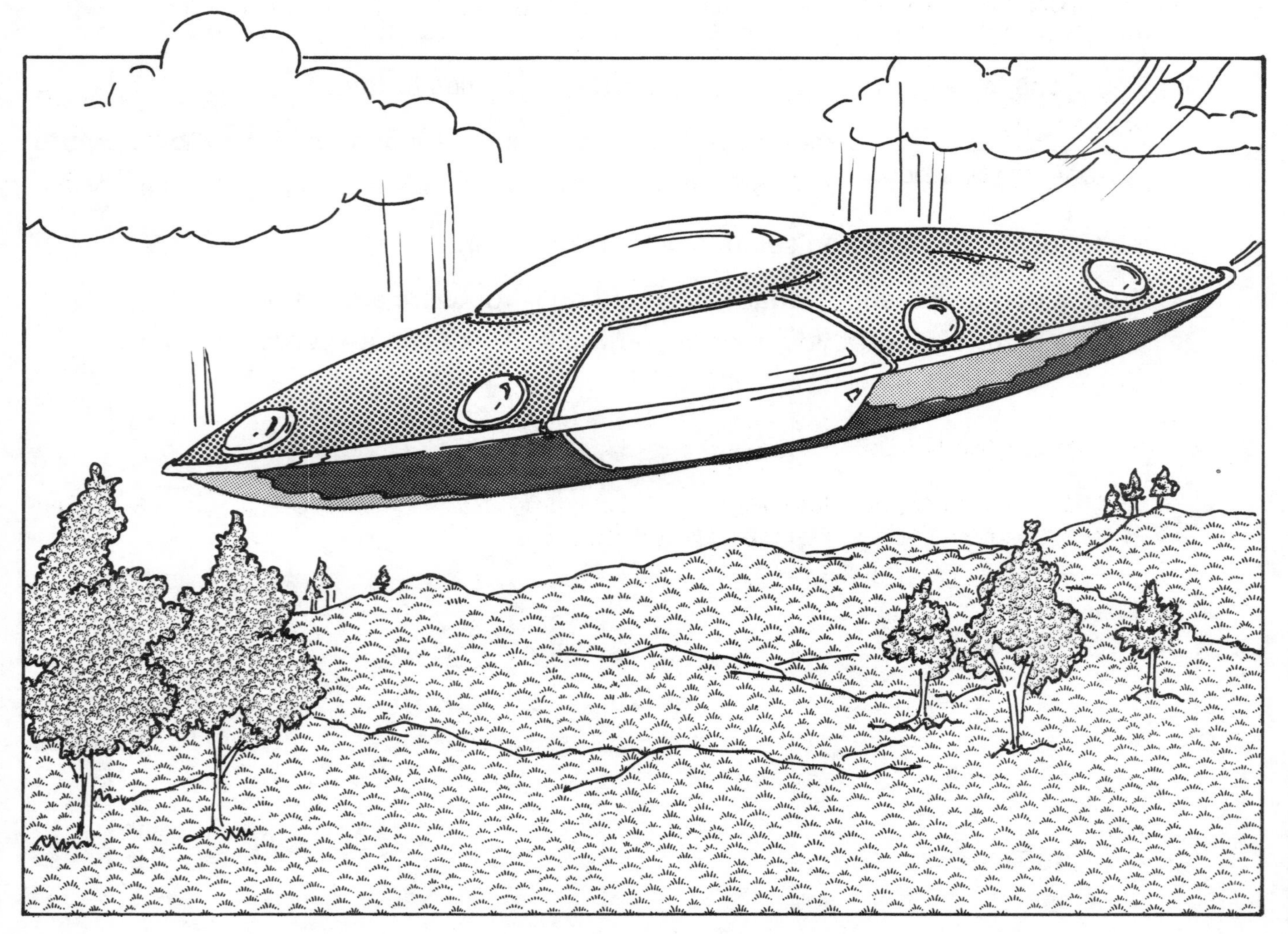

Name ______________________________

extra-

A. Divide the following words so that the prefix meaning "beyond" or "outside" is separate.

Example: extramural extra mural

1. extraordinary ________ ________
2. extracurricular ________ ________
3. extrasensory ________ ________
4. extraterrestrial ________ ________

B. From the word list, select the word that best completes each sentence. Write the word in the blank.

1. Because Pamela's praise for my new outfit was too ____________, I doubted her sincerity.
2. George could never tell a story simply and clearly; he always added mountains of ____________ details.
3. ESP is the abbreviation for ____________ perception.
4. Because my uncle has lived in Europe for many years, his visits are ____________ events.

C. Do the following activities on separate sheets of paper.

1. Tell about a movie you have seen that involved extraterrestrial creatures. Name the movie and write a few sentences about the plot.
2. List five extracurricular activities. Draw a picture of a person engaged in one of them.

geo earth

geode	a globe-shaped hollow stone having a cavity lined with inward-growing crystals
geography	the science that deals with the surface of the earth and its physical features, climates, vegetation, and population distribution
geology	the study of the earth, including its origin, structure, composition, and history
geometry	the branch of mathematics that deals with the properties of figures in space
geothermal	relating to the earth's internal heat

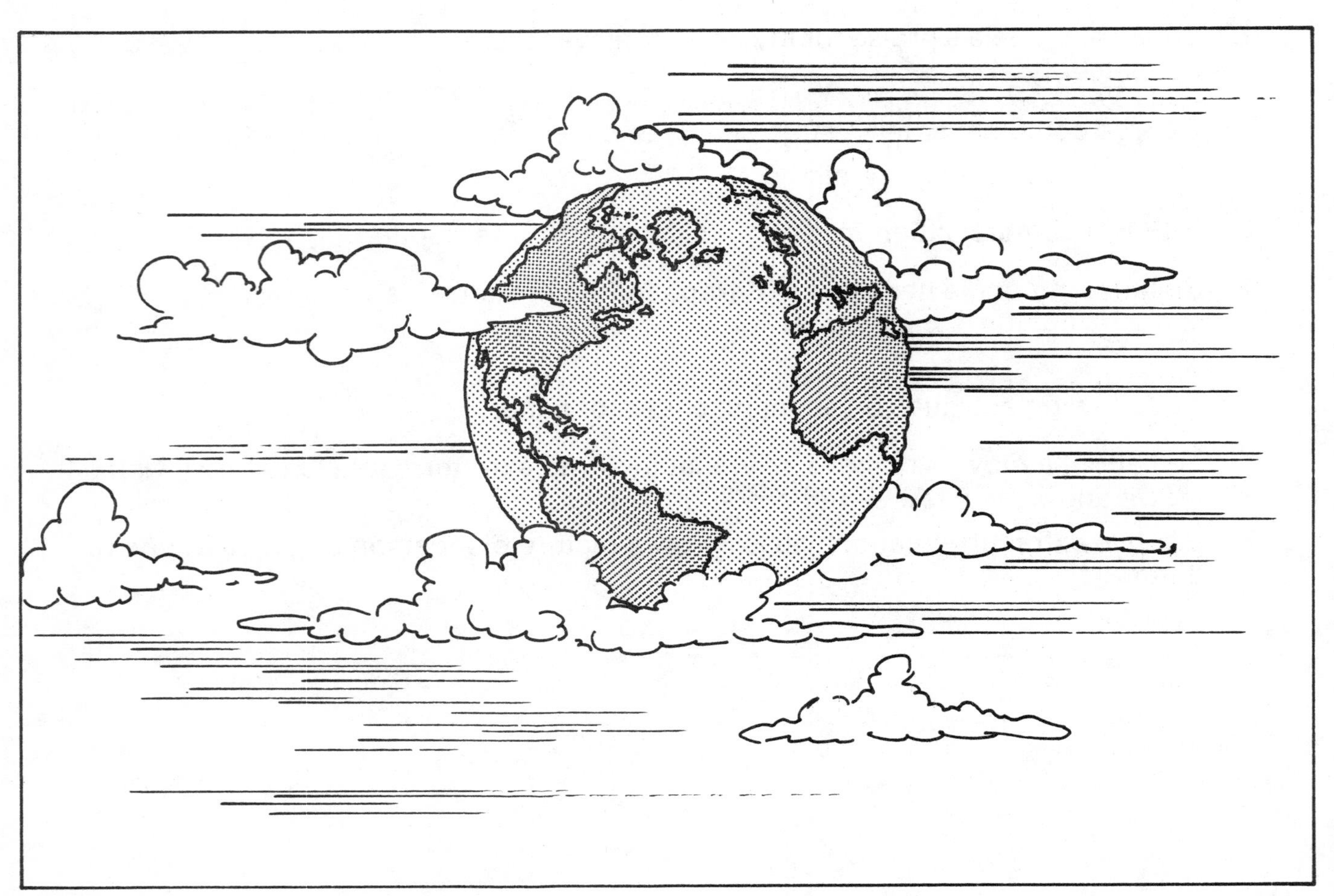

Name ____________________

geo

A. Match each word with its definition. Put the number of the definition in the blank by the word.

____ geology

____ geode

____ geometry

____ geothermal

____ geography

1. The mathematical study of the properties of points, lines, angles, surfaces, and solids
2. A small hollow ball of rock lined inside with crystals
3. Of the heat inside the earth
4. The study of physical features on the earth's surface and the distribution of life on it
5. The study of the physical nature and history of the earth

B. From the word list, select the word that best completes each sentence. Write the word in the blank.

1. Because Pat had developed a serious interest in fossils, she decided she wanted to study ____________________ in college.
2. Its ____________________ is one of the causes of drought and famine in the Sahara region of Africa.
3. Algebra and ____________________ are two branches of mathematics that most high school students study.
4. The prize of Mario's rock collection was a ____________________ that had cracked open.

C. Do the following activities on separate sheets of paper.

1. Name the life forms that existed during these geological periods: Cambrian, Silurian, Devonian, Triassic, Jurassic. Use a dictionary or encyclopedia as a reference.
2. Draw a picture or create a design using only geometric shapes.

graph   to write

calligraphy	the art of fine handwriting
graphic	relating to writing, drawing, or painting; vivid or lifelike
graphite	a soft, black, greasy-feeling form of carbon, used in pencils and as a lubricant
mimeograph	a duplicating machine that uses a type of stencil to reproduce written material
seismograph	an instrument that records earthquake vibrations
stenographer	a person who specializes in taking dictation by shorthand

Name ____

graph

A. Circle the root that means "to write, to draw" in each of the following words.

1. graphic
2. calligraphy
3. seismograph
4. mimeograph
5. stenographer
6. graphite

B. From the word list, select the word that best completes each sentence. Write the word in the blank.

1. It wasn't a very strong earthquake because the ____________________ only showed a reading of 3.1 on the Richter scale.
2. Because photocopiers have become so popular, it's hard to find anyone who still knows how to run a ____________________ .
3. The essential component of a pencil is ____________________ .
4. A skilled ____________________ should be able to take dictation at the rate of 100 words a minute.
5. The reporter's description of how washing machines are made was interesting because it was so ____________________ .

C. Do the following activities on separate sheets of paper.

1. Write the alphabet and your name in calligraphic lettering.
2. Look up the history of stenography, or shorthand, in an encyclopedia. Write a paragraph about it.

Name ____

Review Test 1

A. Circle the root or prefix in each of the following words. Then write the meaning of the root or prefix in the blank after the word.

1. geology ______________________
2. predict ______________________
3. automobile ______________________
4. controversy ______________________
5. antifreeze ______________________
6. asterisk ______________________
7. aqueduct ______________________
8. extraordinary ______________________
9. seismograph ______________________
10. audible ______________________

B. Fill in each blank with the prefix or root that will make a word to fit the definition.

1.	________ate	to say something that will be written down by another person
2.	calli________y	the art of fine handwriting
3.	________nomy	the scientific study of stars and planets
4.	________lung	a device for breathing under water
5.	________thermal	of the internal heat of the earth
6.	________ble	able to be heard
7.	________ry	opposite; perverse
8.	________graph	a person's own signature or handwriting
9.	________sensory	beyond what can be perceived by the senses
10.	________biotic	a substance that kills germs

hyper- over, overly

hyperactive	extremely or abnormally active
hyperbole	a deliberate exaggeration used for effect only
hypercritical	excessively critical; finding too much to criticize
hypertension	abnormally high blood pressure
hyperventilation	extremely rapid or deep breathing that causes dizziness and faintness

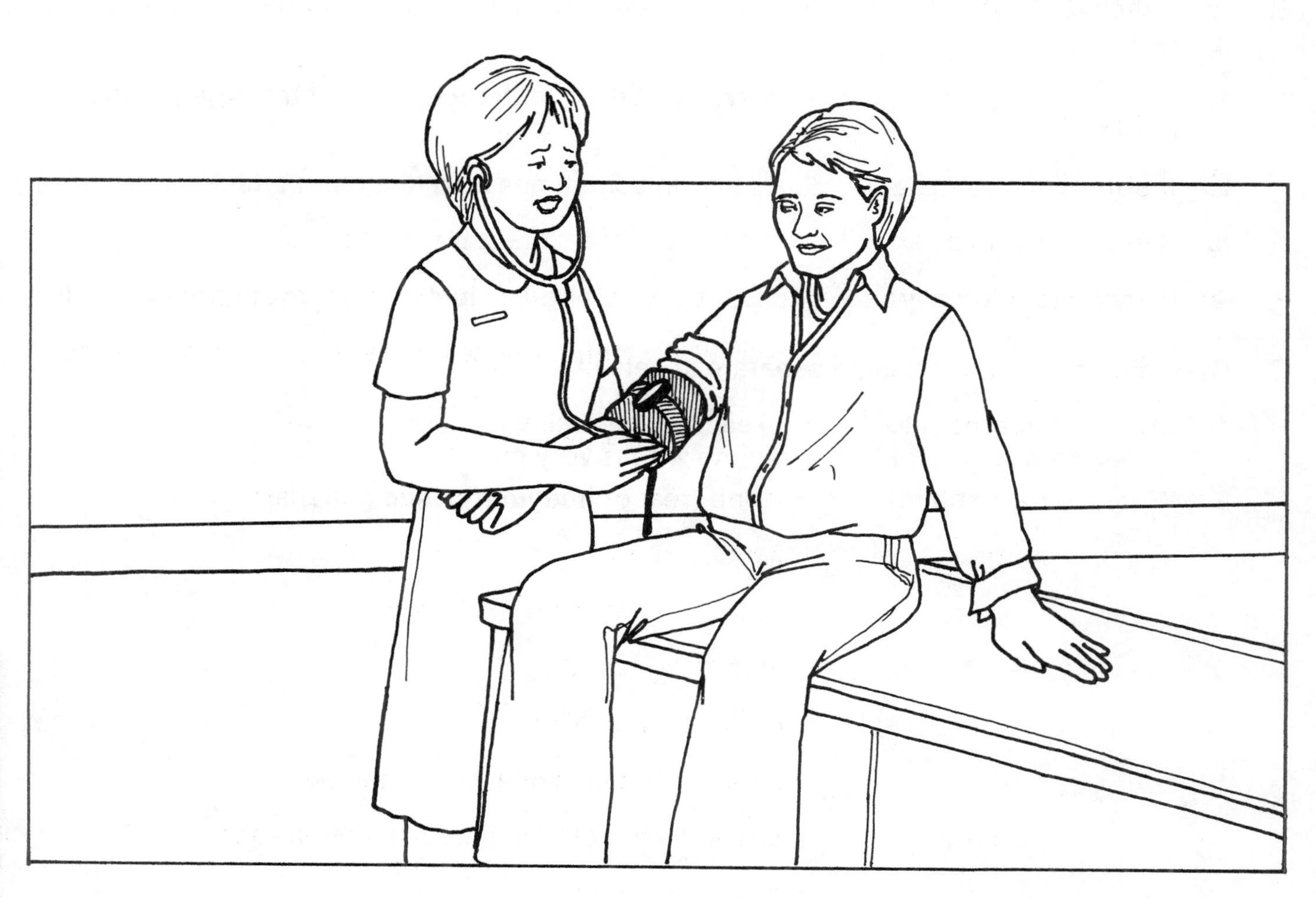

Name ____

hyper-

A. Unscramble these words. Write the correct word next to its meaning.

ntepishenryo **ecavityphre** **chiltriperyca** **beopherly**

1. an exaggeration for effect ____________________
2. unusually high blood pressure ____________________
3. excessively active ____________________
4. finding fault without good reason ____________________

B. From the word list, select the word that best completes each sentence. Write the word in the blank.

1. ____________________ causes dizziness because there is too much oxygen in the blood.
2. If untreated, ____________________ can sometimes lead to a heart attack.
3. "He's as strong as an ox" is an example of a ____________________ .
4. Charlie wasn't really ____________________ ; he was just a very curious five-year-old.

C. Do the following activities on separate sheets of paper.

1. Invent a hyperbole to describe each of the following: someone who is very strong, someone who is very tall, someone who is very mean.
2. Write a paragraph about someone (real or imaginary) who is hypercritical or hyperactive.

-logy   the study of

archeology	the study of the life and culture of ancient people
meteorology	the study of weather
psychology	the study of the human mind and behavior
seismology	the study of earthquakes
theology	the study of religion
zoology	the study of animals

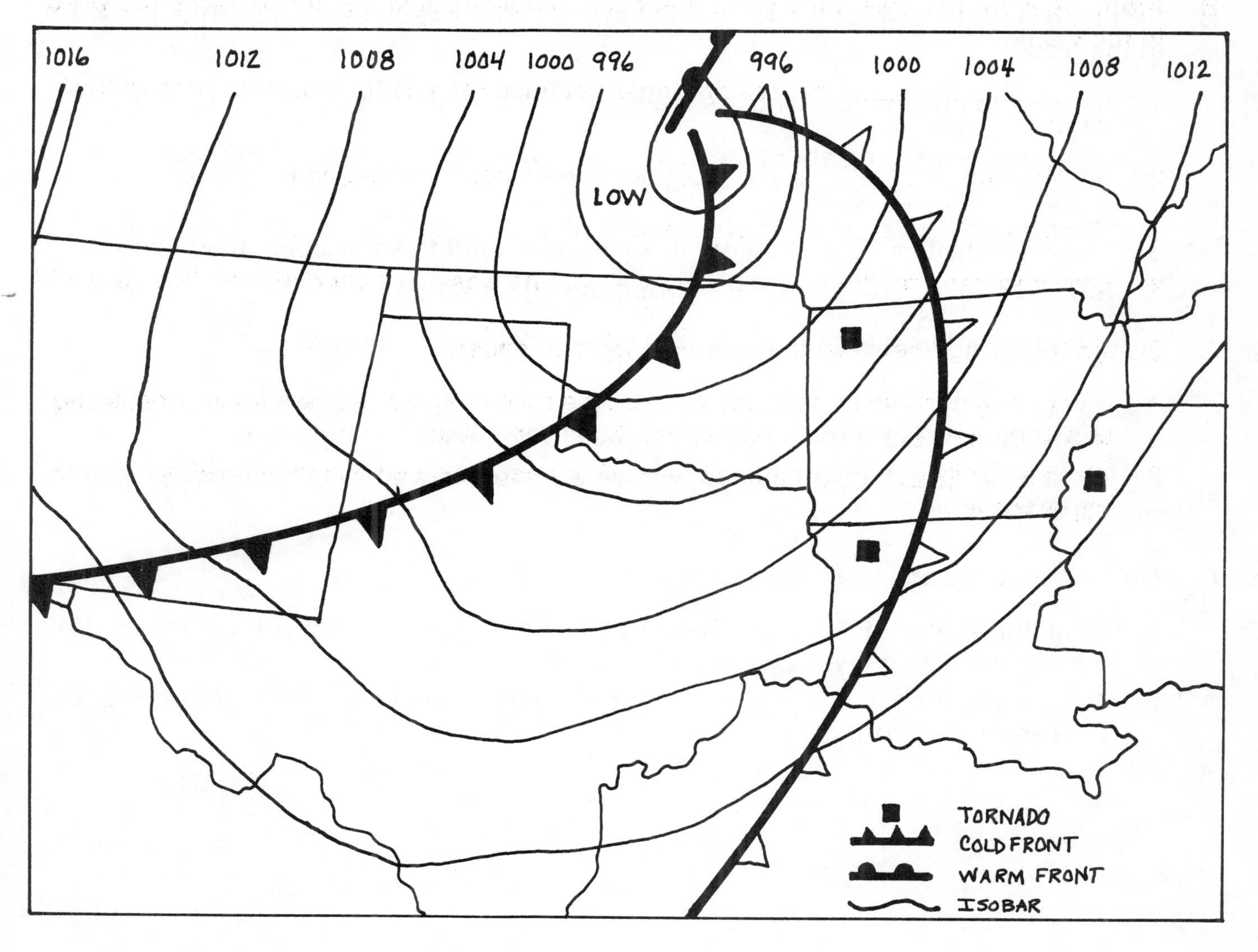

Name ______________________________

-logy

A. A person who studies biology is a biologist. What is a person called who studies the following subjects? Write the word in the blank.

1. zoology ______________________
2. psychology ______________________
3. archeology ______________________
4. meteorolgy ______________________
5. seismology ______________________

B. From the word list, select the word that best completes each sentence. Write the word in the blank.

1. In order to help people who are mentally ill, one must study ______________.
2. If you enjoy learning about life in ancient Egypt, you might try studying ______________.
3. To plan activities for a vacation, it would be helpful to know something about ______________ in order to bring the right clothes.
4. If you are interested in animals, you could take up the study of ______________.
5. If you lived in California, it might be wise to know something about ______________ so that you would understand what was happening when the earth trembled.

C. Do the following activities on separate sheets of paper.

1. Of all the studies defined on the word list, which one interests you the most? Write a paragraph stating your choice and give reasons why.
2. Draw a picture of the workplace of someone who specializes in one of the subjects defined on the word list.

magna, magni	**great, large**

magnanimous — showing great generosity, especially in forgiving injury or insult

magnate — a person who has great power, especially in business

magnificent — presenting great splendor or beauty

magnify — to make something appear larger

magnitude — greatness or importance

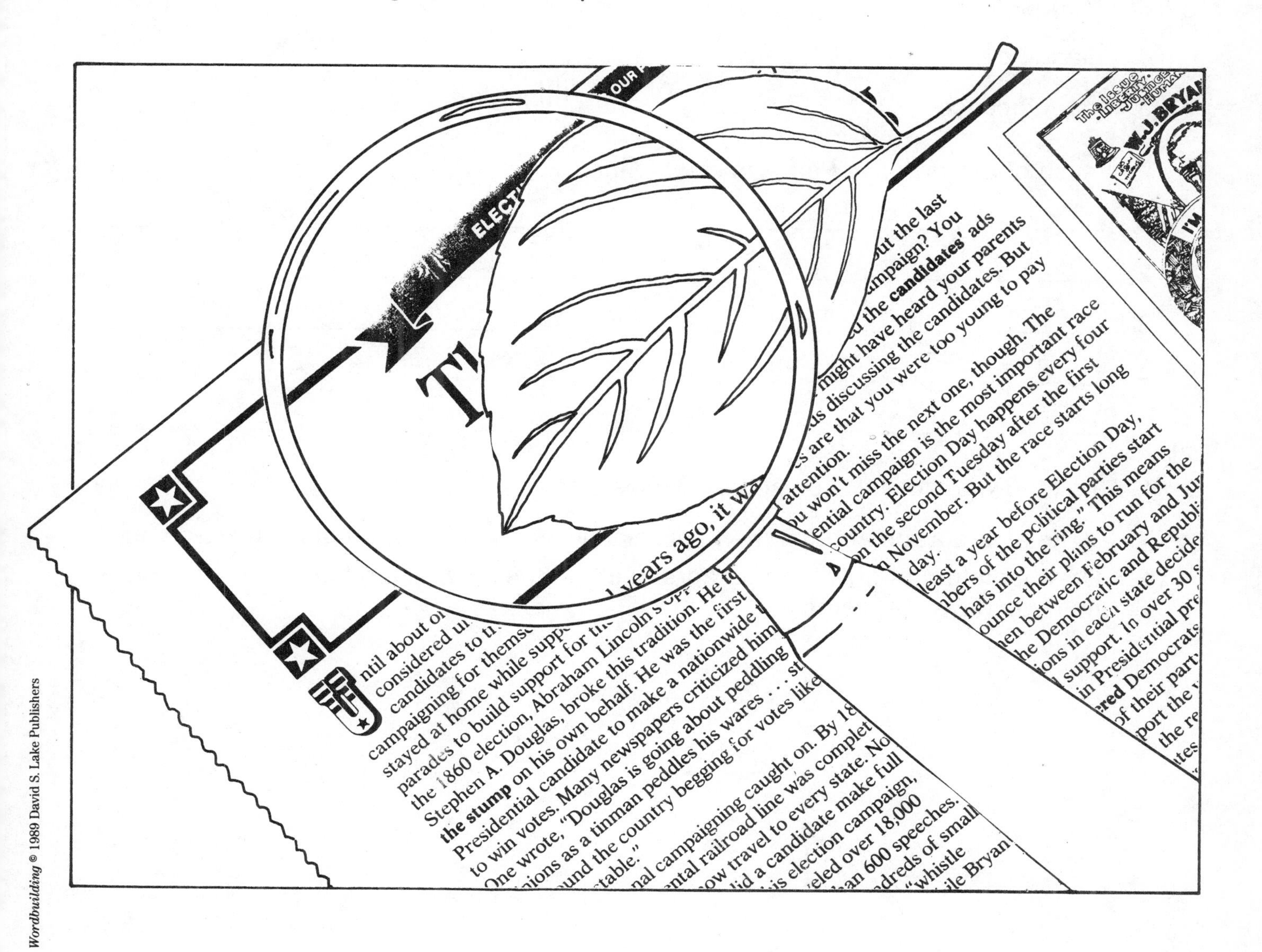

Name ________________________________

magna, magni

A. Name the parts of speech for each of the following words.

Example: magnify *verb*
magnifier *noun*

1. magnification ____________
2. magnanimous ____________
3. magnanimity ____________
4. magnificent ____________
5. magnificence ____________

B. Use each of the words in Part A in a sentence.

1. ________________________________
2. ________________________________
3. ________________________________
4. ________________________________
5. ________________________________

C. Do the following activities on separate sheets of paper.

1. Write a paragraph about a friend or relative who was magnanimous toward you.
2. Draw a picture of or write a paragraph about the most magnificent view in nature that you have ever seen.

man, manu hand

manacle	to put handcuffs on, to restrain *(verb)*; handcuff *(noun)*
manicure	cosmetic care of the hands and fingernails
manipulate	to control or move with the hands; to handle skillfully
manual	done by hand *(adjective)*; a handbook providing information or instruction *(noun)*
manufacture	to make a product by hand or by machinery
manuscript	a handwritten or typed copy of an article, book, or report before it is printed

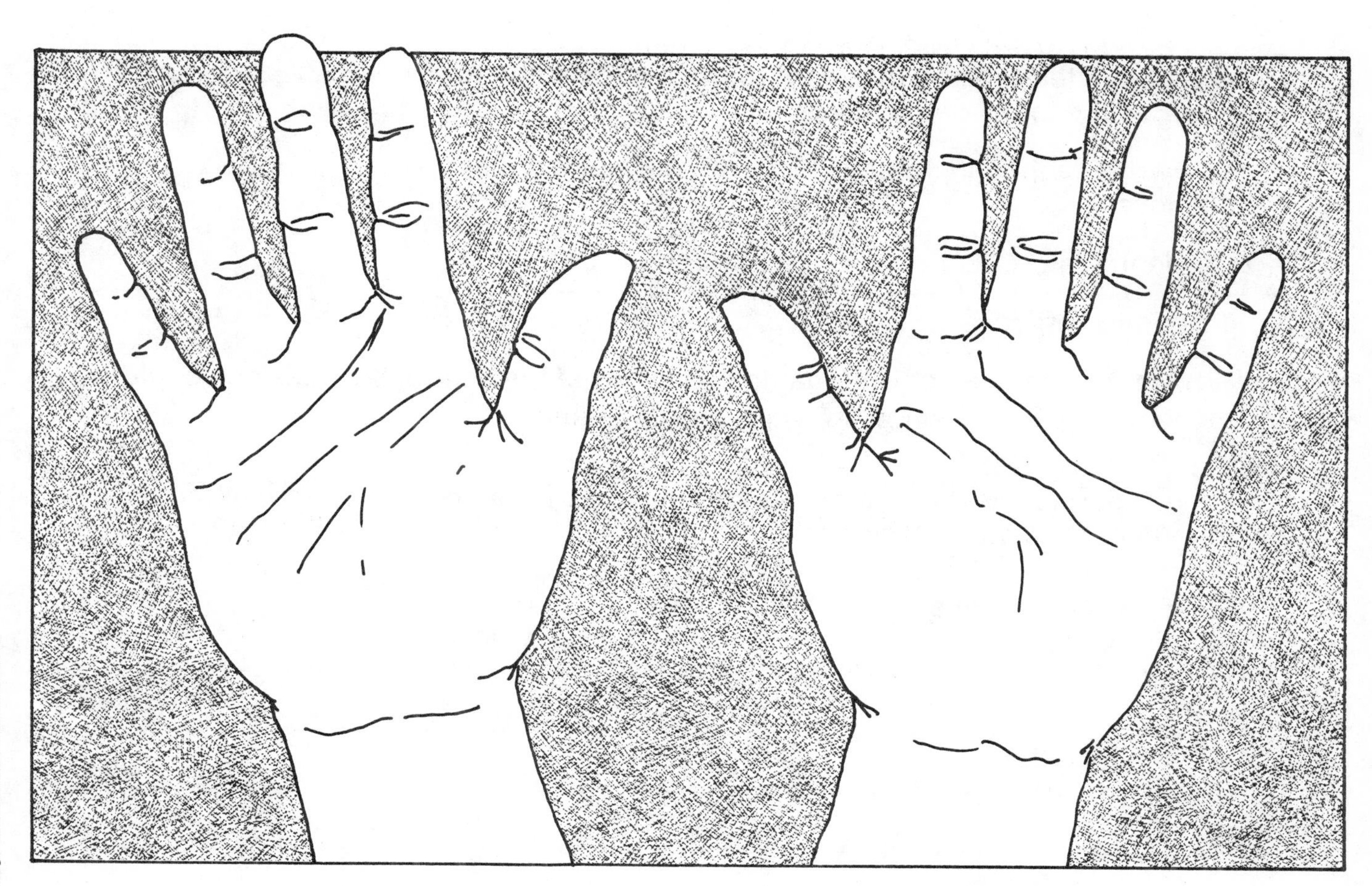

Name ______________________________

man, manu

A. Circle the root that means "hand" in each word below. Then define the word in the blank. Refer to the word list or use a dictionary.

Example: manufacturer a company that makes products

1. manacled ______________________________
2. manipulation ______________________________
3. manually ______________________________
4. manicurist ______________________________

B. From the word list, select the word that best completes each sentence. Write the word in the blank.

1. After I painted the house, I went to the beauty salon for a ______________ to improve the looks of my hands.
2. The writer sighed in relief as he wrote the last word of the ______________ for his novel.
3. Carpentry is ______________ labor.
4. The police officer ______________(d) the criminal.
5. Roxanne was the electronic-game champion of the school because she could ______________ the controls so skillfully.

C. 1. On a separate sheet of paper, design the cover for a manual about manicuring or manufacturing some product.

2. List four manual jobs.

____

____

____

____

metr, meter — to measure

barometer	an instrument used for measuring atmospheric pressure to forecast weather
meter	an instrument used to measure something; the basic unit of length in the metric system
metronome	an instrument that sounds an adjustable number of musical beats per minute
speedometer	a device used for measuring the speed of and distance traveled by a vehicle
trigonometry	a branch of mathematics studying the relationships between angles and sides of triangles and other figures

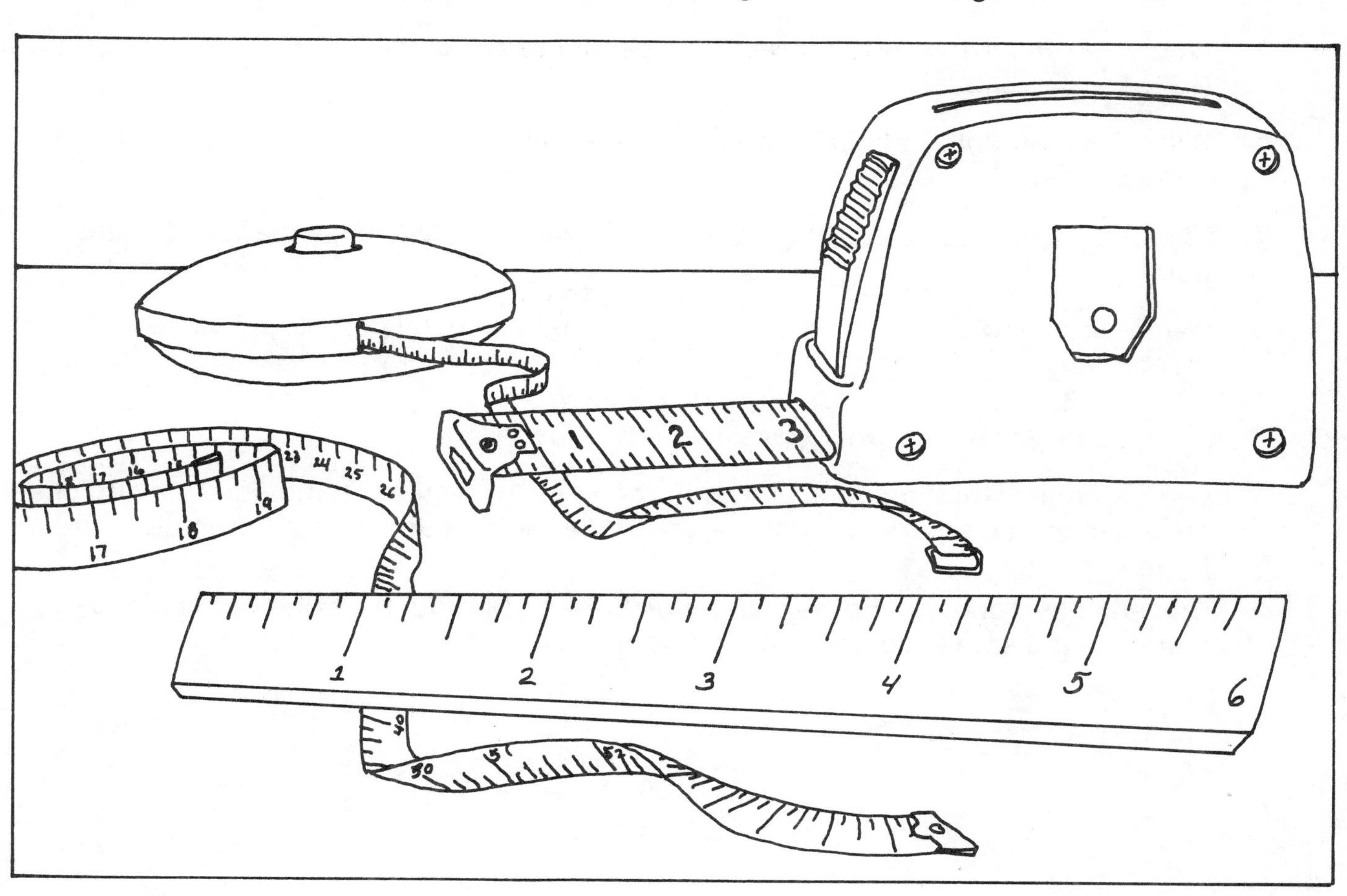

Name ____

metr, meter

A. Circle the root that means "to measure" in the following words.

1. trigonometry
2. metronome
3. barometer
4. speedometer

B. From the word list, select the word that best completes each sentence. Write the word in the blank.

1. We had to watch the time while we were shopping so we could get back to the car before the time ran out on the parking ________________.
2. One of the instruments that a weather forecaster relies on is the ________________.
3. When I was learning to play the piano, I had to use a ________________ to keep a steady beat.
4. The ________________ indicated that we were maintaining a steady 55 miles per hour.
5. Before studying ________________, you must usually complete courses in algebra and geometry.

C. Do the following activities on separate sheets of paper.

1. Draw a picture that includes at least three kinds of meters. Some possible choices are a gas meter, a parking meter, a speedometer, a pedometer, a barometer, and a thermometer.
2. Use an encyclopedia or other reference book to find out how one of the kinds of meters listed above works. Write a paragraph about it.

multi- many

multicolored	having many colors
multimedia	combining more than two artistic techniques or means of communication or expression, such as acting, lighting effects, and music
multimillionaire	a person who has at least two million dollars
multiple	having many parts or elements
multitude	a large number of persons or things

Name ______________________________

multi-

A. Unscramble the word and write the definition.

Example: limptule _multiple_ _having many parts or elements_

1. rollutimedoc ____________ ____________
2. lemonlimitailiur ____________ ____________
3. demiltutu ____________ ____________
4. immediatul ____________ ____________

B. From the word list, select the word that best completes each sentence. Write the word in the blank.

1. The unhappy result of John's skiing accident was a ____________ fracture of the arm.
2. A kaleidoscope is constructed with ____________ glass.
3. The rock concert with television screens and a light show was a ____________ event.
4. A ____________ donated money for the starving children.
5. The ____________ of people followed the celebrity into the theater.

C. Do the following activities on separate sheets of paper.

1. Draw a multicolored multitude.
2. Write a paragraph about what you would do with your money if you were a multimillionaire.

ped foot

biped	an animal having two feet
centipede	a long, many-segmented insect with a pair of legs on each segment
pedestal	the foot or bottom support of a statue, column, or other object
pedestrian	a person who travels on foot; a walker
pedicure	cosmetic care of the feet and toenails
pedometer	an instrument that measures distance walked by recording the number of steps

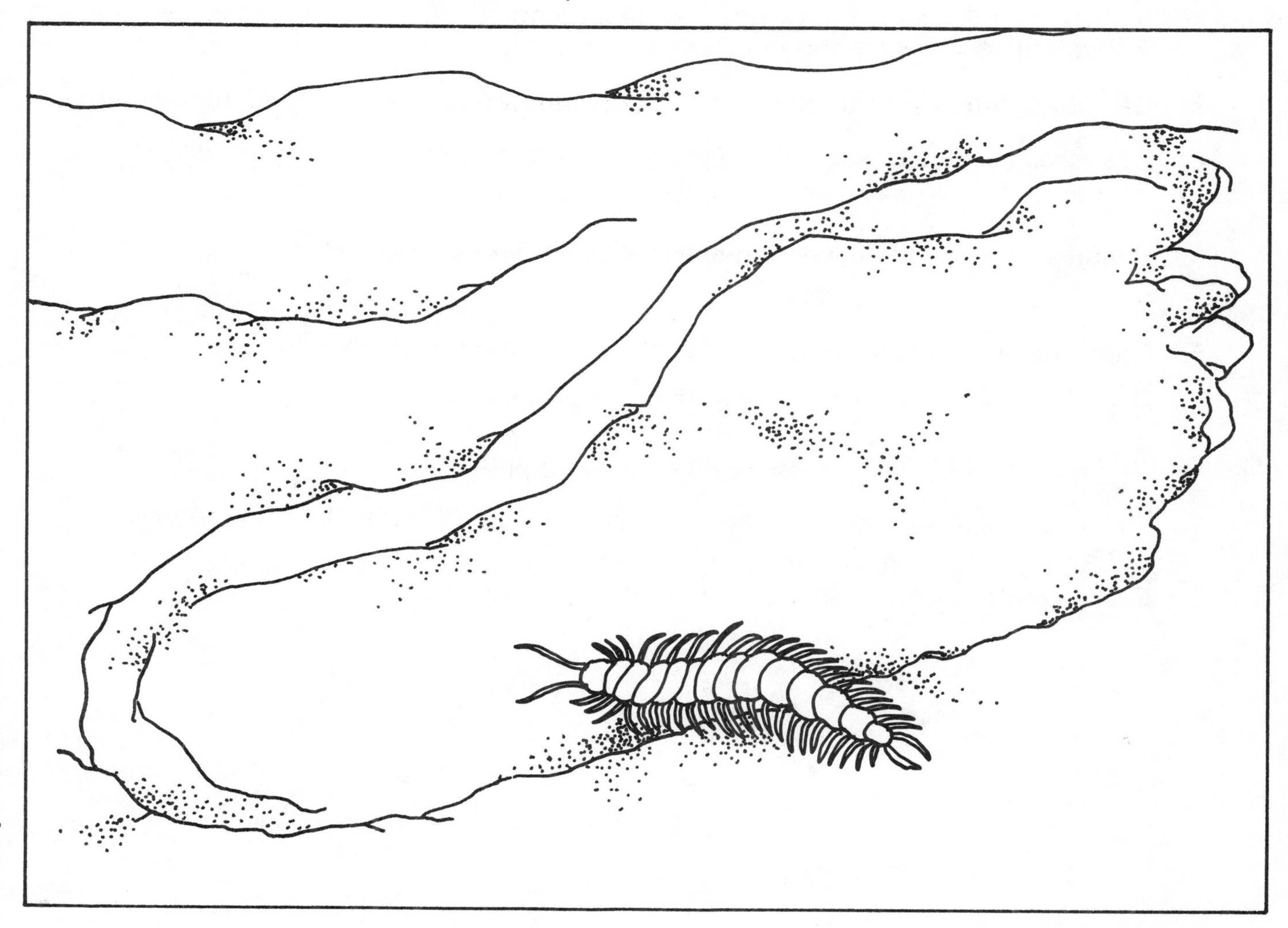

Name ______________________________

ped

A. Fill in the word from the word list that matches the meaning.

1. a person who is on foot ____________
2. a two-footed animal ____________
3. the base of a statue ____________
4. cosmetic care of the feet and toenails ____________
5. an instrument that records distance walked ____________

B. From the word list, select the word that best completes each sentence. Write it in the blank.

1. A flamingo is like a person because it is a ____________ .
2. Cars sometimes ignored the ____________-crossing lines at intersections.
3. Ellen was curious to know how far she walked in a day, so she decided to carry a ____________ .
4. Because she would be wearing sandals during the summer, Samantha usually got a ____________ in May.
5. Harry teased his sister by claiming she had as many pairs of shoes as a ____________ has pairs of feet.

C. Do the following activities on separate sheets of paper.

1. Write a paragraph about the farthest distance you have traveled as a pedestrian. Where were you going? How long did it take?
2. Draw a picture with a biped, a centipede, and a pedestal in it.

phon, phone sound

megaphone	a funnel-shaped device for amplifying or directing sound
microphone	an instrument that changes sound waves into electrical signals for transmission or amplification
phonetic	having to do with speech sounds
phonics	the rules of sound used in teaching reading and word pronunciation
xylophone	a percussion instrument consisting of tuned wooden bars struck with small hand-held hammers

Name ______________________________

phon, phone

A. Circle the root that means "sound" in the following words.

1. phonetic
2. xylophone
3. phonics
4. megaphone
5. microphone

B. From the word list, select the word that best completes each sentence. Write the word in the blank.

1. When you cup your hands around your mouth so that someone at a distance can hear you better, you are imitating a ______________.
2. Jeff brought his tape recorder in for repairs because the ______________ wasn't working.
3. The dictionary uses ______________ symbols to show how words are pronounced.
4. The drum, the glockenspiel, and the ______________ are all percussion instruments.

C. Do the following activities on separate sheets of paper.

1. Find the pronunciation key in a dictionary. Make a list of the phonetic symbols used for the vowel sounds and the words used to demonstrate each sound. Then add a second word that uses each vowel sound.
2. Draw a picture that includes a megaphone, a microphone, and a xylophone.

post- after

postdate	to date with a future date
postgraduate	relating to studies beyond the level of a bachelor's degree
postpone	to put off to another time, to delay
postscript	a sentence, note, or paragraph added to a letter after the signature
postwar	after a war

Today my
went to the planetarium
It was really fun.

We are decorating for my birthday party this weekend. We are going to put up streamers and balloons. Mom baked a cake. It has a blue flower car on it.

Sincerely,
Jason

P.S. I hope I get a football for my birthday. I asked Mom and Dad for a bike, a remote control car, and a football. I really want the football.

Name ______________________________

post-

A. Unscramble these words. Write the correct word next to its meaning.

ttdeasop **stcopstrip** **rawpots** **ppotsoen** **dragtepuosat**

1. of studies for a master's or doctor's degree ____________
2. after a war ____________
3. delay ____________
4. a note at the end of a letter ____________
5. to date afterward ____________

B. From the word list, select the word that best completes each sentence. Write the word in the blank.

1. Because there were many more interesting things to do, Gloria would usually ____________ doing her homework until the very last minute.
2. The ____________ baby boom began in 1945 when U.S. soldiers returned from the war zones in Europe and the Pacific Ocean.
3. Henry decided to ____________ the check because the store could not deliver the sofa until next week.
4. After he signed the letter, Alan realized that he had forgotten the most important news, so he added a ____________ about his new bike.
5. Because Gabrielle wanted to be a doctor, she knew she would not only have to complete four years of college, but she would also have to do several years of ____________ work.

C. 1. Write a letter to a friend or relative on a separate sheet of paper. After you sign it, add a postscript. Mail your letter after the teacher has checked it.

2. Name three professions that require postgraduate work.

____

____

____

pre- before

preamble	a statement that introduces a formal document, explaining its purpose
precede	to come or go before in rank, time, or order
prehistoric	of the period before written history
preoccupied	wholly occupied or absorbed in one's thoughts; absentminded
preschool	school before kindergarten; nursery school
prevent	to take action before an event to stop the event from happening

Name ______________________________

pre-

A. In the first blank, name the part of speech for each of the following words. In the second blank, give a short definition.

Example: prehistoric *adjective* *of the period before written history*

1. precede ________ ____________________
2. precedent ________ ____________________
3. preoccupation ________ ____________________
4. prevention ________ ____________________
5. preventable ________ ____________________

B. From the word list, select the word that best completes each sentence. Write the word in the blank.

1. The four-year-old child will attend a ______________ class.
2. The dinosaurs lived during ______________ times.
3. The teacher said we had to memorize the ______________ to the United States Constitution.
4. Roger couldn't enjoy the movie because he was ______________ about the test the next day.
5. Seventh grade ______________(s) eighth grade.

C. Do the following activities on separate sheets of paper.

1. Use a dictionary to find five other words that begin with the prefix *pre-* (meaning "before"). List the words and their meanings.
2. Draw a picture of what a prehistoric preschool might have looked like.

Name ______________________________

Review Test 2

A. Circle the root or prefix in each of the following words. Then write the meaning of the root or prefix in the blank after the word.

1. magnify ______________________
2. postdate ______________________
3. pedicure ______________________
4. manual ______________________
5. hypercritical ______________________
6. barometer ______________________
7. phonics ______________________
8. psychology ______________________
9. prevent ______________________
10. multiple ______________________

B. Fill in each blank with the prefix or root that will make a word to fit the definition.

1.	speedo________	an instrument for measuring speed
2.	mega________	a cone-shaped device for amplifying sound
3.	________active	excessively active
4.	________icure	cosmetic care of the hands and fingernails
5.	________estrian	a person traveling on foot
6.	________historic	of the period before recorded history
7.	zoo________	the study of animals
8.	________ficent	having great splendor or beauty
9.	________colored	having many colors
10.	________pone	to put off until later

re- again

rearrange	to place in a new way
recede	to move back or farther away; to slope backward
recondition	to put into good condition again; to repair
reconsider	to think about again, particularly when being asked to change a decision
redecorate	to change the style and appearance, usually of a room or a home
regress	to return to an earlier or less mature level of development

Name ______________________________

re-

A. Sometimes a *re-* word can have two different meanings. Then you need to use a hyphen to show the difference. For example, *recover* means "to get (something) back." But if the meaning you want is "to cover again," you need to add a hyphen: *re-cover*. When there is a hyphen, *re-* always means "again." Define the following pairs of *re-* words.

release ______________________________

re-lease ______________________________

repay ______________________________

re-pay ______________________________

resign ______________________________

re-sign ______________________________

return ______________________________

re-turn ______________________________

B. From the word list, select the word that best completes each sentence. Write the word in the blank.

1. Dorothy said no at first, but later she wanted to ______________ her answer.
2. He would have to ______________ his bicycle if he wanted to sell it.
3. When the two of them got together, they seemed to ______________ to behaving like three-year-olds.
4. The strip of wet sand at the water's edge showed how much the tide had ______________(d).
5. Ethan would have to ______________ his plans if he wanted to go to the party, too.

C. Do the following activities on separate sheets of paper.

1. Draw a picture of how you would rearrange and redecorate your room if you had an unlimited amount of money.
2. Write a paragraph describing a situation in which you or someone else reconsidered or regressed.

scope — to look

horoscope	an analysis of the position of stars and planets at a particular place and time
kaleidoscope	a tube-shaped toy that one looks through to see a variety of changing colored patterns
microscope	an optical instrument for viewing objects too small to be seen by the naked eye
periscope	an optical instrument for viewing objects that are overhead or otherwise out of sight—used especially in submarines
scope	range of view or understanding; the space within which something exists, covers, or is limited to

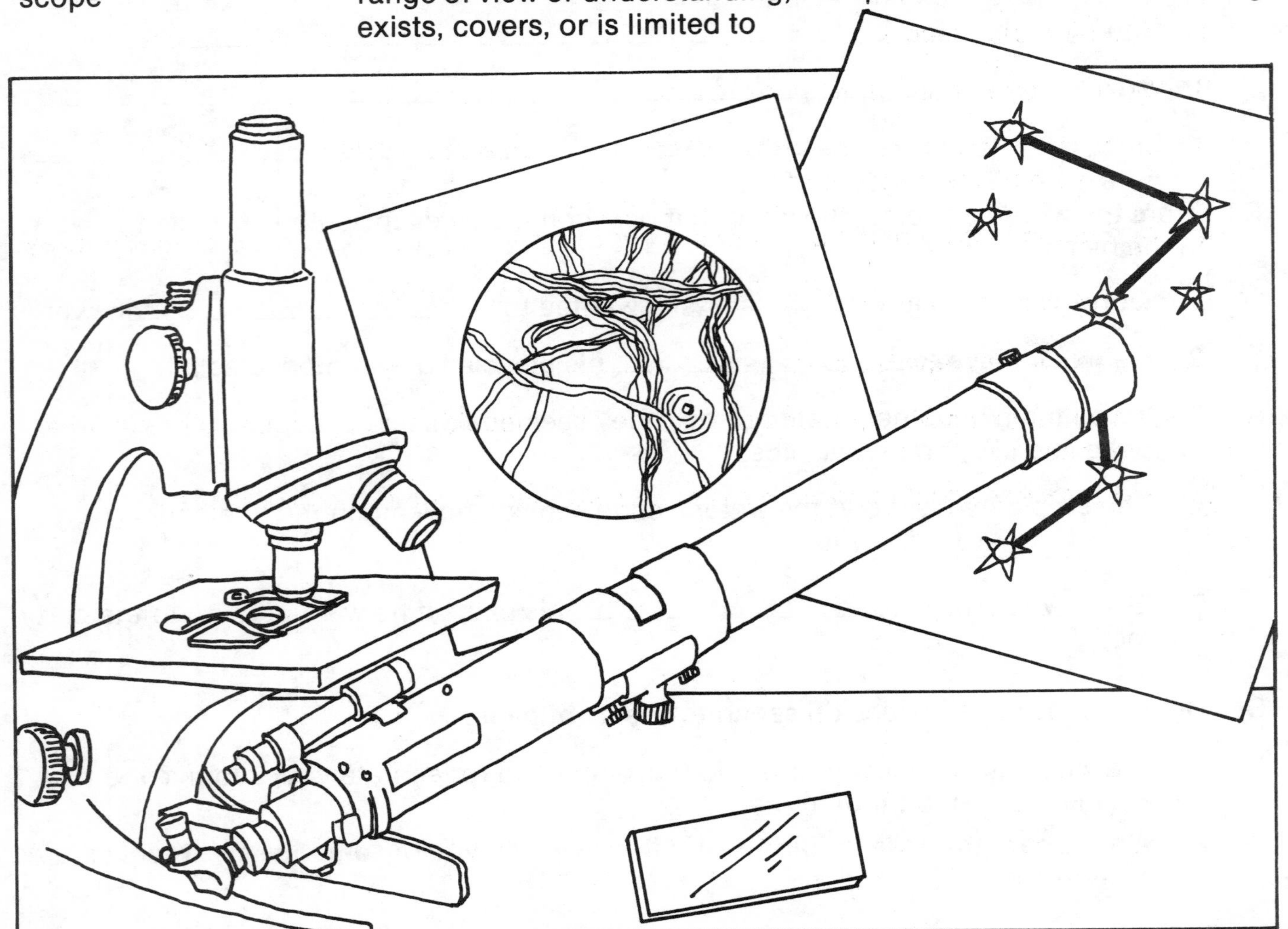

Name ____________________

scope

A. What do each of these "scopes" show you? Write the number of the view in the correct blank.

___ kaleidoscope	1. the position of stars and planets at a given time
___ microscope	2. objects that are overhead or otherwise out of view
___ horoscope	3. colored patterns
___ periscope	4. extremely small objects

B. From the word list, select the word that best completes each sentence. Write the word in the blank.

1. The biologist used a ________________ to help with her research.
2. Jerry enjoyed the colors and patterns in his ________________ .
3. Once the submarine was under water, the crew relied on the ________________ to see what was on the surface.
4. A detailed history of the periscope is out of the ________________ of a dictionary.
5. A ________________ is often used to predict the future.

C. Do the following activities on separate sheets of paper.

1. Draw and color what you might see through a kaleidoscope, a microscope, and a periscope.
2. List ten things that cannot be examined without the aid of a microscope.

scrib, scrip — to write

inscribe	to write, mark, or engrave words or symbols on some surface
prescription	written instructions from a doctor for the preparation of a particular medicine or remedy
scribble	to write or draw hastily and carelessly; to make meaningless marks or lines
scribe	a person who copied manuscripts before the invention of the printing press; a writer or author
script	handwriting; a copy of the text of a stage, radio, or television show
superscript	something written above and to the side of a number, letter, or word

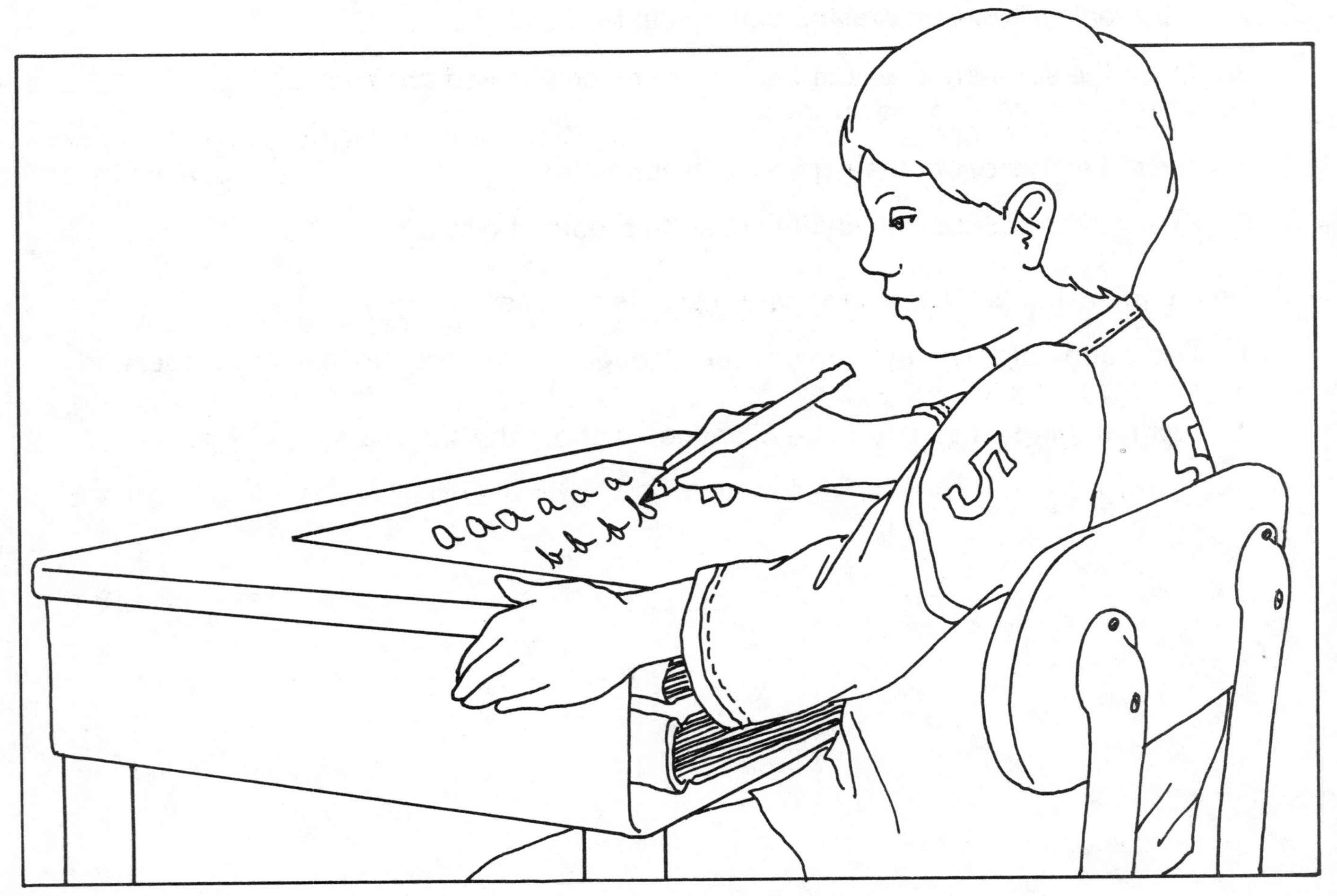

Name ______________________________

scrib, scrip

A. In each of the following words, circle the root that means " to write."

1. scribe
2. inscribe
3. script
4. prescription
5. superscript
6. scribble

B. From the word list, select the word that best completes each sentence. Write the word in the blank.

1. The doctor has given his patient a ________________ .
2. The director went over the ________________ with the cast.
3. Because Cara had ________________(d) her phone number, I couldn't call her with the homework assignment she had missed.
4. The jeweler asked her whose initials she wanted him to ________________ on the locket.
5. Many ________________(s) were skilled in the art of calligraphy.

C. Do the following activities on separate sheets of paper.

1. Write the first ten lines of dialogue for a script of a TV show or a movie.
2. Draw a picture that includes three objects with names or initials inscribed on them.

spec to see, to look at

aspect	the look or appearance of anything
introspective	examining one's own thoughts and feelings
specimen	a single part or thing used as a sample or example of a whole group
spectacle	anything viewed or seen; a public performance
spectator	a person who watches an event
spectrum	the range of colors visible to the human eye; a continuous range or entire extent

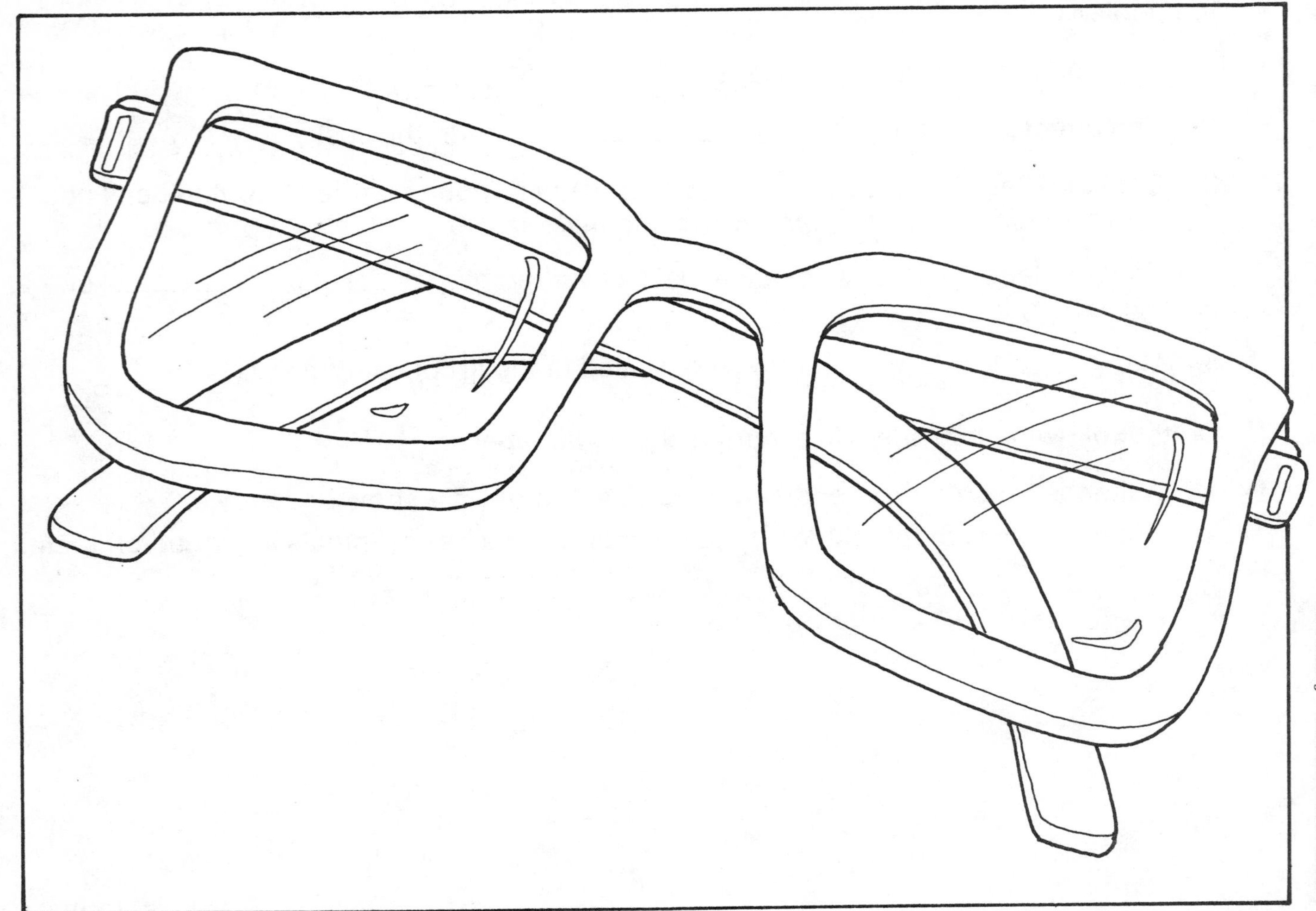

Name ________________________________

spec

A. Unscramble these words. Write the correct word next to its meaning.

calcepest **casttrope** **pacset** **victorinestep** **mesnepic**

1. the way a person or a thing looks ______________
2. a typical part or example ______________
3. looking into one's own mind and feelings ______________
4. something to look at ______________
5. an onlooker ______________

B. From the word list, select the word that best completes each sentence. Write the word in the blank.

1. The circus advertised itself as the greatest ______________ in the world.
2. No one realized he was ever ______________, because he always seemed so self-confident.
3. The investigator asked for a ______________ of everyone's handwriting.
4. You can find the whole ______________ of types in our school—from preppie to punk.
5. In bruising games like football and soccer, I'd rather be a ______________ than a participant.
6. Elsie's whole ______________ reflected what an absolutely terrible week it had been.

C. 1. Look up *spectrum* in a dictionary or encyclopedia. On another sheet of paper, use crayons, colored pencils, or felt-tip markers to show the spectrum of color.

2. What is a spectator sport?

____

List four spectator sports.

______________ ______________

______________ ______________

sub- under, below, less than

subconscious	existing in the mind below the level of conscious awareness
subject	to bring under the power of another *(verb)*; an area of knowledge to be studied or a topic to main theme *(noun)*
submarine	a ship designed and equipped to operate under water
submerge	to place under water or other liquid
subterranean	lying beneath the earth's surface; underground
subtotal	the total of part of a series of numbers

Name ______________________________

sub-

A. Unscramble these words. Write the correct word next to its meaning.

grusmeeb **lastbout** **mearnbius** **bossucuscion** **bestcuj**

1. to bring under some power or influence ______________
2. a total that is part of a final total ______________
3. to plunge under a liquid ______________
4. a ship designed to travel on and under water ______________
5. existing below the level of conscious awareness ______________

B. From the word list, select the word that best completes each sentence. Write the word in the blank.

1. Geometry was not Andy's favorite ______________ .
2. The explorers descended carefully into the ancient ______________ cave.
3. Before tax was added, the ______________ was $12.98.
4. Calling his aunt by his sister's name was a ______________ slip of the tongue.
5. The crew of the ______________ didn't look forward to the long days of being totally closed in under tons of water.
6. I like a bath only if the water is deep enough for me to completely ______________ myself.

C. Do the following activities on separate sheets of paper.

1. Draw a submerging submarine. On another sheet of paper, draw the submarine's captain and his captor, to whom he is subject.
2. What would life be like if we lived in a subterranean civilization? Write a paragraph about one aspect of life underground.

super- above, over, more than

superficial	of or on the surface; not deep or thorough
superhuman	exceeding ordinary human power or ability
superior	high or higher in degree, rank, order, or quality
supernatural	not belonging to the natural world; miraculous
supervise	to direct or oversee an activity; to be in charge

Name ______________________________

super-

A. Give the part of speech and a short definition of each word.

Example: supervise ___verb___ ___to direct or oversee an activity___

1. supervision ________ ________________________
2. supervisor ________ ________________________
3. superficial ________ ________________________
4. superficially ________ ________________________
5. superior ________ ________________________
6. superiority ________ ________________________

B. From the word list, select the word that best completes each sentence. Write the word in the blank.

1. The wrestler lifted the heavy crates with ______________ strength.
2. The coach will ______________ the football squad's training.
3. He claimed he was a computer expert, but his knowledge was really only ______________ .
4. The haunted house was supposed to be filled with ghosts and other ______________ creatures.
5. The regulars at the tennis courts spent hours arguing about which type of racket was ______________ .

C. Do the following activities on separate sheets of paper.

1. Draw a picture with three supernatural creatures in it.
2. Have you ever seen someone do something that seemed to be a superhuman feat? Write a paragraph about it.

tele- far

telecommunication	the science or technology of communicating sounds, signals, or pictures by wire or radio
telegraph	a system for sending coded messages from a transmitter to a receiver
telephoto	a magnifying camera lens used to photograph distant objects
telescope	an optical instrument that makes distant objects appear nearer and larger
teletypewriter	a form of telegraph in which messages to be sent are typed out and reproduced by an automatic typewriter on the receiving end

Name ______________________________

tele-

A. Divide the following words into two parts so that the prefix meaning "far" is separate.

Example: television *tele* *vision*

1. telescope ________ ________
2. telegraph ________ ________
3. telephoto ________ ________
4. telecommunication ________ ________
5. teletypewriter ________ ________

B. From the word list, select the word that best completes each sentence. Write the word in the blank.

1. Morse code is the "language" used by the ______________ .
2. Observatories use giant ______________(s) to look at the stars.
3. A ______________ is often found in newspaper offices because whole stories, rather than brief messages, must be transmitted.
4. Before the invention of the telephone and the radio, the field of ______________ did not exist.
5. The photographer used a ______________ lens for the pictures of the lions because he had no desire to get very close.

C. Do the following activities on separate sheets of paper.

1. Look up the Morse code in an encyclopedia. Write your name in Morse code. Then write a paragraph comparing the telegraph and the telephone as means of communication.
2. On one sheet of paper, draw a scene. On a second sheet of paper, draw a part of that scene as it would look through a telephoto lens or a telescope.

terr, terra   earth, ground

terrace	one of a series of raised strips of land that rise one above the other; an open, outdoor living area connected to a house
terrain	the shape or features of the surface of a piece of land
terrarium	a small enclosure, often of glass, for keeping small land animals or growing plants
terrestrial	relating to the earth or land
territory	any land, region, or district, especially that controlled by a particular nation or ruler

Name ______________________________

terr, terra

A. Match each of the following words with its definition. Put the number of the definition on the blank by the word.

____ terrestrial	1. any of a series of flat platforms of earth rising one above the other
____ territory	2. the surface features of a tract of land
____ terrace	3. a glass box in which small land animals and plants are kept
____ terrarium	4. of land or the earth
____ terrain	5. a region, district, or area of land

B. From the word list, select the word that best completes each sentence. Write the word in the blank.

1. The explorers noted the ________________ of the new lands.
2. Seaweed is not a ________________ plant.
3. The new owners of the house wanted to add a ________________ .
4. In science class, we set up a ________________ for the chameleon.
5. The pioneers were given permission to explore and settle the new ________________ owned by Great Britain.

C. Do the following activities on separate sheets of paper.

1. Write a paragraph describing what you consider to be your territory.
2. Draw a terrarium. Include a lizard, crickets, grass, and plants in it.

un- not

undesirable	not pleasant; objectionable
unearned	not gained by work or service; not deserved
unequal	not the same in extent, quantity, rank, or ability
unforgettable	never to be forgotten; memorable
unproductive	not productive; producing little
unqualified	not having the necessary or desirable qualifications; total or absolute

Name ______________________________

un-

A. Circle the words that use *un-* as a prefix meaning "not" (or "the opposite of" before a verb, such as *untie*).

unadvisable	unimaginable	unplug
unanimous	uninvited	unshaken
unbind	unique	unsure
uncaring	unity	untangle
unconscious	unknown	until
underage	unlit	untiring
unicycle	unlock	unwind
uniform	unnamed	unworkable

B. From the word list, select the word that best completes each sentence. Write the word in the blank.

1. The children were so well-behaved that Jordan felt that the babysitting money was practically ____________________ .
2. If you haven't already studied the material, last-minute cramming for a test will probably be ____________________ .
3. Norman realized that he'd be ____________________ for a lot of interesting jobs unless he got some computer training.
4. Mona spent the summer on the beach, trying to overcome what she considered to be the ____________________ paleness of her skin.
5. The children worked hard to make sure that their mother would have an ____________________ birthday.
6. Although the quarter and the peso are nearly the same size, they are of ____________________ value.

C. Do the following activities on separate sheets of paper.

1. Draw a picture of the most unforgettable person you ever met. Then write a few sentences explaining why that person is unforgettable.
2. Write a paragraph about a situation in which you or someone else received either unearned blame or unearned praise.

vis — to see, to look

invisible	cannot be seen
revise	to read over carefully and then correct or improve as necessary; to change
visor	the projecting front brim of a hat that shades the eyes; the movable part of the helmet of a suit of armor that can be lowered to cover the upper part of the face
vista	a view, especially a distant one seen through an opening or along a passage
visualize	to form a mental image of something

Name ______________________________

vis

A. Draw a circle around the root that means "to see" or "to look" in each word below. Then briefly define each word on the blank beside it.

1. visor ______________________________
2. invisible ______________________________
3. vista ______________________________
4. revise ______________________________
5. visualize ______________________________

B. From the word list, select the word that best completes each sentence. Write the word in the blank.

1. The pitcher adjusted the ________________ on his cap as a signal to the catcher.
2. We pulled off the road to get a better look at the breathtaking ________________ .
3. Careful students don't hand in the first draft of an important paper; they take the time to ________________ .
4. Close your eyes and try to ________________ the face of a friend you haven't seen for a long time.
5. The secret message was written in ________________ ink.

C. Do the following activities on separate sheets of paper.

1. What is the first thing you would do if you were invisible? Write a paragraph about it.
2. Draw a picture of a knight with a visor on his helmet and a baseball player with a visor on his or her cap. Show both of them standing in front of an invisible vista.

Name ____________________

Review Test 3

A. Circle the root or prefix in each of the following words. Then write the meaning of the root or prefix in the blank after the word.

1. telephoto ____________________
2. kaleidoscope ____________________
3. introspective ____________________
4. scribble ____________________
5. revise ____________________
6. supernatural ____________________
7. unequal ____________________
8. terrestrial ____________________
9. recondition ____________________
10. submarine ____________________

B. Fill in each blank with the prefix or root that will make a word to fit the definition.

1. micro________	an instrument for looking at very small objects
2. ________rium	a small glass enclosure for plants and small land animals
3. in________ible	cannot be seen
4. super________	a letter or number above and to the side of a word
5. ________consider	to consider again
6. ________desirable	objectionable
7. a________	the way something or someone looks
8. ________conscious	existing below the level of conscious awareness
9. ________vise	to oversee
10. ________graph	an instrument for transmitting messages over a distance

Name ____________________

Final Test

A. Circle the correct answer in each sentence below.

1. *Un* in *unequal* means **same as** **less than** **not.**
2. *Anti* in *antiseptic* means **against** **toward** **very.**
3. *Extra* in *extravagant* means **beyond** **overly** **against.**
4. *Multi* in *multitude* means **heavy** **many** **colorful.**
5. *Aqua* in *aquaplane* means **blue** **fast** **water.**
6. *Terra* in *terrarium* means **brown** **land** **slow.**
7. *Logy* in *archeology* means **the study of** **the measurement of** **writing.**
8. *Ped* in *pedestal* means **toe** **foot** **hand.**
9. *Post* in *postgraduate* means **before** **to send** **after.**
10. *Graph* in *calligraphy* means **to see** **to write** **to measure.**

B. Define the word in the first blank. Then put the meaning of the prefix and the root in the next two blanks.

Example: *Audiometer* means an instrument to measure hearing because *audi* means to hear and *meter* means to measure.

1. *Contradict* means ____________________
   because *contra* means ____________ and *dict* means ____________.
2. *Telegraph* means ____________________
   because *tele* means ____________ and *graph* means ____________.
3. *Postscript* means ____________________
   because *post* means ____________ and *script* means ____________.
4. *Pedometer* means ____________________
   because *ped* means ____________ and *meter* means ____________.

5. *Supervise* means ______________________________

because *super* means ______________ and *vis* means ______________.

6. *Geology* means ______________________________

because *geo* means ______________ and *logy* means ______________.

7. *Predict* means ______________________________

because *pre* means ______________ and *dict* means ______________.

8. *Revise* means ______________________________

because *re* means ______________ and *vis* means ______________.

C. Circle the prefix and underline the root in each of the following words. Then give the meaning of the prefix and the root in the blanks.

Example: (tele)vise = far + to see

1. astrology = ______________ + ______________
2. extraterrestrial = ______________ + ______________
3. manuscript = ______________ + ______________
4. subscript = ______________ + ______________
5. geometry = ______________ + ______________
6. autograph = ______________ + ______________
7. audiovisual = ______________ + ______________
8. telescope = ______________ + ______________

D. Fill in the blank in each sentence with one of the words listed below.

antidote asterisk controversy extraneous hypertension
magnanimous meteorology precede recede spectrum
subtotal superficial terrain visualize

1. Fortunately, the cut was not deep; it was only ______________.
2. The doctor consulted a medical dictionary for an ______________ for the poison.
3. He was worried that as he got older, his hairline would ______________.

4. I had a hard time following the story because she added so many ________________ details.

5. Although he was disappointed by his defeat, Ernest made the ________________ gesture of reaching across the net to shake hands with his opponent.

6. A rainbow contains the entire color ________________ .

7. An ________________ is a symbol often used for footnotes.

8. Exercise and a healthy diet can help to control ________________ .

9. In the alphabet, M ________________(s) N.

10. To add up several long columns of numbers, it is advisable to find the ________________ of each column and add them together.

11. A weather forecaster must study ________________ .

12. The proposed dress code created a lot of ________________ in our school.

13. To answer that question on the science test, Georgia tried to ________________ the experiment.

14. The ________________ made the spot a perfect campsite: a level area underneath some trees with a stream nearby.

Answer Key

Pretest, page 7

1. against
2. water
3. star
4. to hear
5. self
6. opposite
7. to write
8. beyond
9. earth
10. to write
11. overly
12. the study of
13. large
14. hand
15. to measure
16. many
17. foot
18. sound
19. after
20. before
21. again
22. to look
23. to write
24. to see
25. below
26. more than
27. far
28. earth
29. not
30. to see

anti-, page 9

A. The circled words are anticlimax, antidemocratic, antifreeze, antigravity, antipoetic, antiseptic, antisocial, antisymmetric

B. 1. antiaircraft; 2. antifreeze; 3. antisocial; 4. antibiotic; 5. antidote

C. Answers will vary.

aqua, aque, page 11

A. 1. aqua marine
2. aqua lung
3. aqua plane
4. aque duct

B. 1. aqualung; 2. aquarium; 3. aquatic; 4. aqueduct; 5. aquaplane

C. Answers will vary.

aster, astro, page 13

A. 3. astronaut
4. astrology
2. asterisk
5. asteroid
1. astronomy

B. 1. astronomer; noun
2. astronautics; noun
3. astrologer; noun

C. 1. Asteroids have orbits between Mars and Jupiter.

Solar System

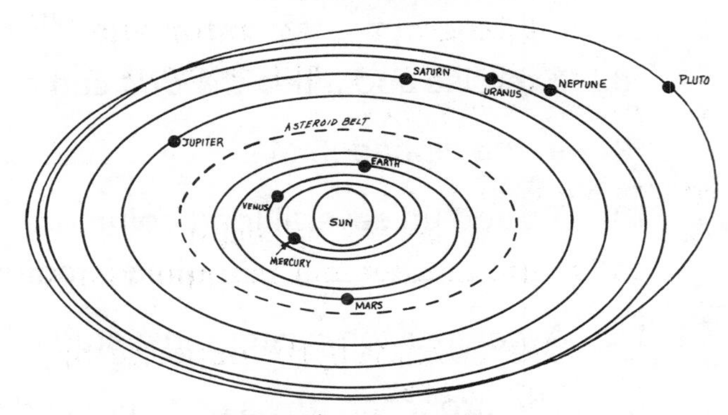

2. Answers will vary.

audi, page 15

A. 1. audiovisual: involving the use of both sight and sound
2. auditory: having to do with hearing
3. audible: loud enough to be heard
4. auditorium: a large theater or concert hall
5. audition: a trial performance in which a musician or actor is heard and evaluated

B. 1. auditorium; 2. audiovisual; 3. audition; 4. audible.

C. 1.

Ear

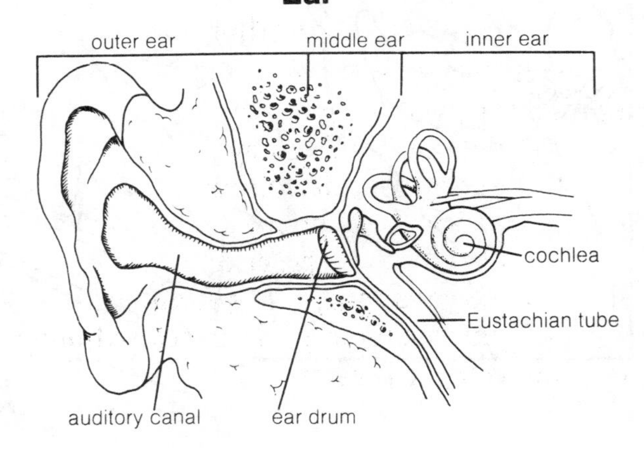

2. Answers will vary.

auto-, page 17

A. 1. noun
2. adjective
3. adjective
4. adverb
5. adjective
6. noun

B. 1. autobiography; 2. automatic;
3. autograph; 4. autonomous

C. Answers will vary.

contra, contro-, page 19

A. 1. verb; to say the opposite
2. noun; a statement in opposition to another
3. adjective; saying the opposite, or inconsistent
4. noun; a difference of opinion
5. adjective; causing disagreement

B. 1. controversy; 2. contraband;
3. contrary; 4. contradict

C. 1. The weather is hot.
The pizza is cold.
The dress is new.

C. 2. Answers will vary.

dict, page 21

A. 1. diction
2. predict
3. dictator
4. verdict

B. 1. verdict; 2. diction;
3. dictate; 4. predict

C. Answers will vary.

extra-, page 23

A. 1. extra ordinary
2. extra curricular
3. extra sensory
4. extra terrestrial

B. 1. extravagant; 2. extraneous;
3. extrasensory; 4. extraordinary

C. Answers will vary.

B. 1. extravagant; 2. extraneous;
3. extrasensory; 4. extraordinary

C. Answers will vary.

geo, page 25

A. 5. geology
2. geode
1. geometry
3. geothermal
4. geography

B. 1. geology; 2. geography;
3. geometry 4. geode

C. 1. *Cambrian:* first animals with shells and skeletons; all animals lived in water, especially trilobites and brachiopods. *Silurian:* first land plants; coral reefs in seas; first jawed fish. *Devonion:* many land plants, including large trees; many kinds of primitive fish; first sharks, insects, and amphibians. *Triassic:* ferns and cycads were dominant plants; ammonites, clams, snails; first dinosaurs; first mammals. *Jurassic:* cycads, gingkoes, horsetails were common plants; reptiles dominant on land, in sea, in air; first bird; a few mammals.
2. Answers will vary.

graph, page 27

A. 1. graphic
2. calligraphy
3. seismograph
4. mimeograph
5. stenographer
6. graphite

B. 1. seismograph; 2. mimeograph;
3. graphite; 4. stenographer;
5. graphic

C. 1. Answers will vary.
2. Answers will vary somewhat but may include the following facts.

Systems to rapidly transcribe the spoken word date from ancient times. Timothy Bright introduced the first modern system in 1588. Isaac Pitman's system of geometric symbols with variations in shading, slope, and outline was introduced in 1837 and is still in use. John Robert Gregg introduced business shorthand in 1888; its curved outlines resemble ordinary script. Some systems, such as Speedwriting, use shortened forms of longhand. Keyboard machines are used to write shorthand in courts of law.

Review Test 1, page 28

A. 1. geology: earth
2. predict: to say
3. automobile: self
4. controversy: against
5. antifreeze: against
6. asterisk: star
7. aqueduct: water
8. extraordinary: beyond, outside
9. seismograph: to write
10. audible: to hear

B. 1. dictate
2. calligraphy
3. astronomy
4. aqualung
5. geothermal
6. audible
7. contrary
8. autograph
9. extrasensory
10. antibiotic

hyper-, page 30

A. hypertension, 2
hyperactive, 3
hypercritical, 4
hyperbole, 1

B. 1. hyperventilation;
2. hypertension; 3. hyperbole;
4. hyperactive

C. Answers will vary.

-logy, page 32

A. 1. zoologist
2. psychologist
3. archeologist
4. meteorologist
5. seismologist

B. 1. psychology; 2. archeology;
3. meteorology; 4. zoology;
5. seismology

C. Answers will vary.

magna, magni, page 34

A. 1. noun
2. adjective
3. noun
4. adjective
5. noun

B. Answers will vary.

C. Answers will vary.

man, manu, page 36

A. 1. manacled: wearing handcuffs
2. manipulation: skillful handling of something or someone
3. manually: by hand
4. manicurist: a person who gives cosmetic treatments to people's hands and fingernails

B. 1. manicure; 2. manuscript;
3. manual; 4. manacle(d);
5. manipulate

C. Answers will vary.

metr, meter, page 38

A. 1. trigonometry
2. metronome
3. barometer
4. speedometer

B. 1. meter; 2. barometer;
3. metronome; 4. speedometer;
5. trigonometry
C. Answers will vary.

multi-, page 40
A. 1. multicolored: having many colors
2. multimillionaire: a person who has at least 2 million dollars
3. multitude: a large number of persons or things
4. multimedia: combining more than two artistic techniques or means of expression, such as acting, lighting effects, and music
B. 1. multiple; 2. multicolored;
3. multimedia; 4. multimillionaire;
5. multitude
C. Answers will vary.

ped, page 42
A. 1. pedestrian; 2. biped;
3. pedestal; 4. pedicure;
5. pedometer
B. 1. biped; 2. pedestrian;
3. pedometer; 4. pedicure;
5. centipede
C. Answers will vary.

phon, phone, page 44
A. 1. phonetic
2. xylophone
3. phonics
4. megaphone
5. microphone
B. 1. megaphone; 2. microphone;
3. phonetic; 4. xylophone
C. 1. Answers will vary according to dictionary used.
2. Answers will vary.

post-, page 46
A. 1. postgraduate
2. postwar
3. postpone
4. postscript
5. postdate
B. 1. postpone; 2. postwar;
3. postdate; 4. postscript;
5. postgraduate
C. Answers will vary.

pre-, page 48
A. 1. verb; to come or go before in rank, time, or order
2. noun; a case that serves as a guide in later cases
3. noun; something that absorbs all one's thoughts
4. noun; a means of keeping something from happening
5. adjective; can be stopped from happening
B. 1. preschool; 2. prehistoric;
3. preamble; 4. preoccupied;
5. precede(s)
C. Answers will vary.

Review Test 2, page 49
A. 1. magnify: great, large
2. postdate: after, behind
3. pedicure: foot
4. manual: hand
5. hypercritical: over, overly
6. barometer: to measure
7. phonics: sound
8. psychology: the study of
9. prevent: before
10. multiple: many
B. 1. speedometer
2. megaphone
3. hyperactive
4. manicure
5. pedestrian
6. prehistoric
7. zoology

8. magnificent
9. multicolored
10. postpone

re-, page 51

A. release: to let go
re-lease: to rent again
repay: to pay back
re-pay: to pay a second time
resign: to give up a position
re-sign: to sign again
return: to come back
re-turn: to turn again

B. 1. reconsider; 2. recondition;
3. regress; 4. recede(d);
5. rearrange

C. Answers will vary.

scope, page 53

A. 3. kaleidoscope
4. microscope
1. horoscope
2. periscope

B. 1. microscope; 2. kaleidoscope;
3. periscope; 4. scope; 5. horoscope

C. Answers will vary.

scrib, scrip, page 55

A. 1. (scrib)e
2. in(scrib)e
3. (scrip)t
4. pre(scrip)tion
5. super(scrip)t
6. (scrib)ble

B. 1. prescription; 2. script;
3. scribble(d); 4. inscribe;
5. scribe(s)

C. Answers will vary.

spec, page 57

A. 1. aspect
2. specimen
3. introspective
4. spectacle
5. spectator

B. 1. spectacle; 2. introspective;
3. specimen; 4. spectrum;
5. spectator; 6. aspect

C. 1. The spectrum is red, orange, yellow, green, blue, indigo, and violet.
2. A spectator sport is one that attracts spectators, such as baseball or hockey, as distinct from a sport that involves participation, such as hunting or fishing.

sub-, page 59

A. 1. subject
2. subtotal
3. submerge
4. submarine
5. subconscious

B. 1. subject; 2. subterranean;
3. subtotal; 4. subconscious;
5. submarine; 6. submerge

C. Answers will vary.

super-, page 61

A. 1. noun; management or direction
2. noun; manager or overseer
3. adjective; on the surface or not deep
4. adverb; on the surface or not deeply
5. adjective; high or higher in degree, rank, order, or quality
6. noun; the state of being better, higher, or greater

B. 1. superhuman; 2. supervise;
3. superficial; 4. supernatural
5. superior

C. Answers will vary.

tele-, page 63

A. 1. tele scope
2. tele graph

3. tele photo
4. tele communication
5. tele typewriter

B. 1. telegraph; 2. telescope(s);
3. teletypewriter;
4. telecommunication;
5. telephoto

C. 1.

Morse Code

A •–	J •–––	S •••
B –•••	K –•–	T –
C –•–•	L •–••	U ••–
D –••	M ––	V •••–
E •	N –•	W •––
F ••–•	O –––	X –••–
G ––•	P •––•	Y –•––
H ••••	Q ––•–	Z ––••
I ••	R •–•	
Period •–•–•–	Comma ––••––	

2. Answers will vary.

terr, terra, page 65

A. 4. terrestrial
5. territory
1. terrace
3. terrarium
2. terrain

B. 1. terrain; 2. terrestrial;
3. terrace; 4. terrarium;
5. territory

C. Answers will vary.

un-, page 67

C. The circled words are unadvisable, unbind, uncaring, unconscious, unimaginable, uninvited, unknown, unlit, unlock, unnamed, unplug, unshaken, unsure, untangle, untiring, unworkable

B. 1. unearned; 2. unproductive;
3. unqualified; 4. undesirable;
5. unforgettable; 6. unequal

C. Answers will vary.

vis, page 69

A. 1. visor: a hat's projecting front rim, which shades the eyes
2. invisible: cannot be seen
3. vista: a distant view seen through an opening or along a passage
4. revise: to read over carefully and correct or improve
5. visualize: to form a mental image of something

B. 1. visor; 2. vista; 3. revise;
4. visualize; 5. invisible

C. Answers will vary.

Review Test 3, page 70

A. 1. telephoto: far
2. kaleidoscope: to look
3. introspective: to see, to look at
4. scribble: to write
5. revise: again; to see, to look
6. supernatural: above, over, more than
7. unequal: not
8. terrestrial: earth, ground
9. recondition: again
10. submarine: under, below, less than

B. 1. microscope
2. terrarium
3. invisible
4. superscript
5. reconsider
6. undesirable
7. aspect
8. subconscious
9. supervise
10. telegraph

Final Test, pages 71–73

A. 1. not
2. against
3. beyond
4. many

5. water
6. land
7. the study of
8. foot
9. after
10. to write

B.
1. to say the opposite; against; to say
2. an instrument to transmit messages over a distance; far; to write
3. a note after the end of a letter; after; to write
4. an instrument that measures how far one walks; foot; to measure
5. to oversee or to direct; over; to see
6. the study of the physical nature and history of the earth; earth; the study of
7. to foretell or say ahead of time that something will happen; before; to say
8. to read over carefully and then correct or improve as necessary; again; to look

C.
1. astrology = star + the study of
2. extraterrestrial = beyond + earth
3. manuscript = hand + to write
4. subscript = below + to write
5. geometry = earth + to measure
6. autograph = self + to write
7. audiovisual = to hear + to see
8. telescope = far + to look

D.
1. superficial; 2. antidote;
3. recede; 4. extraneous;
5. magnanimous; 6. spectrum;
7. asterisk; 8. hypertension;
9. precede(s); 10. subtotal;
11. meteorology; 12. controversy;
13. visualize; 14. terrain